A WAR TO REMEMBER

A WAR TO REMEMBER

U.S.S. BOISE CL47

U.S. NAVY ASIATIC FLEET

WORLD WAR II 1942–1945

CHALMERS H. HALLMAN RADIOMAN RM3/C

WRITTEN BY
STELLA MININGER

Writers Club Press
New York Lincoln Shanghai

A War To Remember

Writers Club Press
an imprint of iUniverse, Inc.

For information address:
iUniverse
2021 Pine Lake Road, Suite 100
Lincoln, NE 68512
www.iuniverse.com

ISBN: 0-595-26425-5

Printed in the United States of America

THIS BOOK IS DEDICATED

TO MY BROTHER RICHARD, MY SON CHALMERS II AND

MY BELOVED, DEAREST FRIEND STELLA MININGER

MY JOURNAL

OF

WORLD WAR II

NOVEMBER 22, 1942—DECEMBER 12, 1945

CHALMERS H. HALLMAN

RADIOMAN RM 3/C

U.S.S. BOISE

CONTENTS

Chapter I

WEDNESDAY DECEMBER 26, 1945   10:39 PM

Pearl Harbor was now pretty much a thing of the past. Approximately eleven months in the past, as my friend Dicker Bauman and I were shooting pool in Old Herb's Pool Hall in the nearby town of Pennsburg. Dicker was a short stubby fellow, about the age of twenty. Just the ripe old army age, as we had received our classification of 1-A back in August and daily we would shyly open that little post office box expecting our hand to gently grasp that little yellow draft card of notice to report to our local number 8 board at Collegeville. So, as we cautiously measured our shots, all this helped divert our attention from the game and as I hung up an easy shot to lose the close game, I exclaimed to Dicker, what say we take a little trip to Philadelphia tomorrow and see what the Navy has to offer us. I don't exactly like that infantry deal they give you in the Army, no siree. You see, at the time they were steering more than fifty percent of Army draftees into the fighting section of the army, the infantry, and for us, well, we weren't exactly in a fighting mood and figured, why not get through as easy as you can, if possible.

Old Dicker was a plumber's apprentice and was getting along okay in his game. However, he heard a lot about getting a ship-fitters rating from a few local navy fellows and he seemed very interested, so our plans were all set for eight the next morning. When I got to bed that night, I thought the situation over again and again to myself, me enlisting in the Navy, WOW—what a story to tell my kids! However, it gave me the chills when I thought of it. Why not wait until I take my last army physical and take a chance on flunking out; however, that was a long shot, as I was okay physically, as far as I knew and the thought of marching feet, mud, much more, and the infantry still persisted way back in my mind. Anyhow, the next morning found Dicker and myself speeding along to Philly in my forty-two Chevy. All the way down both of us felt a bit nervous and were not in a very talkative mood, thus silence excelled.

We found the Customs building, which was a center of activity this time of the morning and we shoved our way up to the Navy Recruiting Office. Some old Chief Petty Officer, with more brass marks on his sleeve than I had ever seen before, directed us to a table where we filled out a few forms and other rigamarool. From then on we stood in line for everything, as we became accustomed to in our later Naval life, as that is a better and more fitting word than career. Physical examination, this and that and finally that most important question, "What do you want to enlist in? the regular Navy for six years or the reserve for the duration and six months?" My God, I thought to myself, six years is a mighty long time! I'll take the reserve, I said, in my cocky voice of speech. That's okay kid, said the Chief Petty Officer from behind the desk, we'll take that cockiness out of your voice, not long from now. I just blushed and said, "oh yeah!"

We got back to the old town and couldn't help being a bit proud, as we told the fellows about our going into the Navy. All I needed was my parents' signature affixed to the form I had, which they readily signed after a few moments of hesitation. It was quite a shock as I told them nothing of my pre-meditated Navy enlistment, and a "Well Mom, I'm in the Navy now!" is bound to stir a little ill feeling in one's Mother and Father, especially since I had a brother in the Army.

My signed form was on its way to Philly the same night. I had a few more weeks in the old hometown until my final notice to report for induction. Anyhow, I didn't mind leaving too much, at that time, as the town was proving boring with nothing to break the monotony. I had no steady girlfriend at the time, so I had nothing to loose, as I figured at the time. Hell, the experience should prove interesting and meeting new friends in all my coming travels will be fun. I never thought too much about being shot at or how monotonous it might become after months at sea. No, in my viewpoint it was strictly all gravy for me.

CHAPTER 2

In the few weeks before final induction, I didn't accomplish very much, except throw a whopper of a drunk the last weekend at home. Anyway, it was at home, in a way, Henry Beiler, a good friend of mine, and I motored up to Yale University in New Haven, Connecticut to witness the traditional Yale—Harvard game and I wanted to bid adieu to one of my best friends, Jere Klotz, who was taking up medicine at Yale. As far as that weekend is concerned, I think none of us shall every forget it. Especially Jere, as he was the one who toiled cleaning up the mess we made in his little room on the Yale Campus. However, as he put it later, anything for a future Navy man. Sunday was miserable and we didn't do too much and got an early start for the old town, as I was anxious and felt it my duty to spend the last few days with the family. We made it in the record time of two hours, after a bit of skillful driving on my part.

That big day finally came, after a sleepless night of scheming and imagining. It was Tuesday morning, November the twenty-fourth, as I looked out of my bedroom window to find the weather miserable. The sound of the autos wet tires across the wet macadam road outside and the raindrops against the windowpane gave me a weird feeling inside, combined with the thought of this being the "Big Day!" My mother came upstairs, just before going to work, and kissed me good-by and gave me a little final advice, as she didn't want me to stop in at the factory on the way to Allentown to say good-by, for fear she might have to cry.

I spent the morning and early noon saying so long to friends. I picked up Dicker and we made our way to "Herb's Pool Hall" to shoot a quick last game of eight ball and had a coke for memories sake.

Everything was okay, as we progressed towards Allentown, the three of us, my sister-in-law Laurita who was with us to take the car home. Through Emmaus, down the hill in Allentown, past the Wire Mill as we silently took in the sights we wouldn't see for some time to come. Yes, what beautiful sights, as I found out later, were more appreciative of when you were anchored on some Mediterranean or Pacific Island Ports. This is it, I said, as we stopped at Fifth and Hamilton Streets. So long Sis, see you for Christmas, I said, as I kissed her gently. Take care of the family and that husband of yours. What a swell sister-in-law to have, I said to myself.

CHAPTER 3

The Recruiting Office in the Post Office building was cluttered with utility bags and young men engaged in idle chatter, as we walked in. We mustered in and then were put through a short physical for late venereal developments, I guess. Already they were ordering us around, getting us used to what was in the making, I guess. We waited around until the "Morning Call" photographer arrived and had a group photo taken, as was customary for all Naval enlistees leaving to serve their great country in this time of world conflict and strife. Some 4-F civilians, I guess, directed the group of proud boys to the Lehigh Valley Station and distributed armbands inscribed "Naval Volunteer," which we proudly displayed on our left arms. WOW! Now we really felt like heroes. On the way to Philly we were given a special car and were herded in like cattle, which is definitely customary of the Navy. The fellows were very jubilant, with the exception of a few "homesickers" who quietly meditated over the situation. "Broad Street Station," yelled the conductor and we all filed out of the car. Everyone noticed that armband on our sleeves and it seemed the female sex was already attracted and sensed the feeling that pretty soon he is going to be in that uniform. Anyhow, they gave that whistle of the howling wolf, which at the time was traditional of that sex toward servicemen.

It was about seven P.M. when we walked into some small Café on Market Street for our first meal on the Navy. Naturally it stank!! Then to the "Seaman's Institute" where we went to spend the night before induction in the morning.

Dicker and I went out that night, as we were given our freedom after we got settled. Seeing Duke Ellington at the Earle Theatre and a few beers at Sloppy Joe's proved our last civilian exploits for a long time.

We took a cab, as it was raining, and back to the institute we went, about one A.M. for a good night's sleep, we thought, but no, anything but that. The fellows were having one hell of a time in the room and the guy in charge of the place warned us, if we couldn't shut up, he would call the cops and get us the hell out of there. After the third or fourth warning we settled down for a few hours of snooze time and our last freedom sleep—two hours.

Up early and to the Customs building again, about eight, for our final Oath, which made us a member of the United States Navy. A lot of family, friends, girlfriends and relatives of the boys were jammed into the room where we took our Oath, and never shall I forget those final words after repeating the final induction Oath; "You are now a member of the United States Navy!" To myself, I thought, there's no backing out now!!

Up Market Street, herded in trucks bound for the 30th Street Station. Never had I seen a more vericiferous crowd. By now we knew we were going to the training station at Bainbridge, Maryland. A new camp, the fellows were talking. Hell, I said to Dicker, that should be a pretty good deal, all new equipment and facilities. Quite to the contrary though, as I found out later. Quite!!!

Man, am I homesick already, I said to myself, as I had a hollow feeling in the pit of my stomach, once the train got underway for Perryville. I tried to interest myself in the sites, but no soap. All I could think of was home sweet home. Perryville at last! Just a little spot on the barren landscape. Into the bus and up that long winding road to Bainbridge and through the gate. Right like an animal being caught in a trap, however, the animal definitely has more of a chance.

CHAPTER 4

LIFE AT BAINBRIDGE: So this is Bainbridge, Chalmers! What a God forsaken place that was. I could hear that much by listening to the forced drive of the motor and the spinning truck wheels as we slowly made our way through the eight-inch deep mud. Many new buildings were springing up here and there; however, none seemed completed as yet.

"The receiving building, all men out!" Once inside of the building we were mustered. Now men, as your name is called off, answer by saying "Here Sir!" Always addressing an officer as Sir, said the officer in charge. Collins, Durfrey, and so forth, coming to Kelly the responding answer was "that's me" and than the fire works! You are in the Navy now and all that bullshit about respecting an Officer. I could see some of the boys shake in their pants as the Officers voice became harsh and loud.

It was about two in the afternoon and they finally decided to feed us. Ah, what a beautiful and palatable meal we had. "Horse cock and baked beans," eat heartily men and then, fall in over here, as he gave us directions.

I was pretty tired after a busy afternoon of catching clothing, which were thrown at you after a speedy job of measuring, which consisted only of a glance from the kid behind the counter. Seven o'clock at night found us lined up at the Pea Coat issuing room. Incidentally, we were standing out in the cold and I was freezing, as were the other 119 fellows assigned to this Company.

Hep two, three, four; hep two, three, four, as we marched down the muddy road with our mattress covers loaded with our newly issued clothes, slung over our shoulders toward our barracks number 220, which was practically a mile and a half away. We all wore rubbers and if you weren't fortunate enough to have a pair that didn't fit, well you could just stop every other step to pull your rubbers out of the mud. When I think of that horrible first night, I do get a few laughs. Especially when a kid named Haribison fell on his face in the mud and his bag of clothes right in the mud beside him. Oh well, said the Company Commander in charge of the Company, you can wash them. It will start you off right. I know the kid was aching to come out with "you dirty so and so, or slap him in the face," but he remained quiet as he concluded, it might be more profitable. The barracks at last! At least it had heat in it. After a speech by the Company Commander of the barracks we found a sack and turned in. Boy, I could just picture how much of a job we would have cleaning this barracks.

Hit the deck! Get out of those sacks! echoed through the barracks. Five-thirty A.M. and what an unearthly time to be getting out of bed, said the kid next to me. So we pulled the covers over our heads and caught a few more winks. However, we found out later it paid to be an early bird, compared to the extra duty the late sleepers got. Different details were to be organized before chow to clean up the barracks. I found myself on the window detail, which was not too bad. Anyhow, I picked a window back in the corner to work on and I don't think I ever touched it.

And so was our life for the next month. Scuttlebutt was hot and heavy that we were getting leaves for Christmas, but we found out differently as Christmas Eve rolled around and we were in our sacks at nine o'clock, lights out. However, the chatter kept up for a few hours, as we ignored threats from the Company Commander to get us out on the drill field if we didn't shut up.

We were in a month now and we felt like old timers, and what a slow month that was. Everyday seemed like a week. No woman had we seen in a month, so Dicker and I decided the time has come that we shall find out more about Bainbridge. Some fellows had been telling us about the reception building. The place where relative, family friends and girl-friends could come on certain days to visit with their boys in camp. Anyhow, Christmas afternoon found us looking over the array of women in the place. They all looked good, and we did have a good time talking to them, if that was all.

CHALMERS H. HALLMAN

RADIOMAN 3/C

CHAPTER 5

It was early in January now and men were being weeded out of our Company for further schooling. I had signed up for radio as my choice of work in the Navy. Why? I don't know! I guess because a pal of mine was in the same work and had told me it was a pretty good racket, and soft work was for me, definitely!

Anyhow, around January 10, 1943 I found out I had been selected as one of an emergency draft of three from our Company who were slated to go to the fleet radio school in Auburn, Alabama. WOW! After seven weeks of "Boot" training at "Bainbridge," Maryland, that was wonderful news for me.

However, all it meant to me was that I had a leave coming up and was I in a jubilant mood, for a while anyhow. At least until I found out that this was an emergency draft and no leave could be given. But they told us after radio school you'll get your back-leave, maybe twenty or thirty days. I felt pretty bad, but gradually consoled myself with the thought that I was getting out of this hell-hole and boot camp to say nothing of a promised long leave after radio school. After the hustle and bustle of getting ready, packing, etc., we hung around the barracks for two full days waiting for the final order to shove off. It finally came and it meant good-by to the old hole at Bainbridge and I said to myself, may I never see this place again. However, as we shall find out near the end of the script, I was very happy to see it again.

It was ten o'clock at night when we finally boarded the buses at the outgoing center and entrained finally at Perryville for our long and slow journey to Auburn, Alabama.

Everyone was happy, because they were glad to be, what we classed as being free again after having a fence around you for six weeks. Now, how the Navy transports its men is something that possibly no one will ever figure out. It took us the sum of four grueling days in day coaches to reach Auburn.

In charge of the draft was some loud-mouthed Chief who tried to keep us happy with his sea stories. Undoubtedly, he had never seen any more salty water than in the old Salt Lake in Salt Lake City, which happened to be his home. Undoubtedly, he was one of the biggest bull shitters I'd seen in the Navy.

We stopped off in Cincinnati and Cleveland, Ohio and later in Atlanta, Georgia.

Now in Atlanta the Chief in charge decided to bring a little color to the city. As we had a few hours layover before entraining for Auburn, he decided a little march through the city might be a nice thing. Upon the suggestion, he received grumbles, growls and all that stuff, but he was not to be argued with and we marched! We were indeed very glad to entrain again! And how! Last leg of the journey and next stop Auburn, Alabama. We had been wearing our heavy pea coats all the way down and the weather was becoming very warm. Auburn and all hands off. We were met at the station by a couple of Chiefs from the radio school as was customary for all incoming drafts.

Well, we're here! Went through my thoughts. All kinds of questions went through my mind as we marched from the station to the school. Just how long I'd last was a very dubious question in my mind.

Hell, I couldn't even pound a typewriter, which was very helpful in this work, but I'd guessed they would teach you. We arrived in Auburn on a Friday and that meant no school on Saturday, but as all incoming drafts were quarantined to the school grounds for a few days after arrival, we had a lot of time to become acquainted.

CHAPTER 6

LIFE AT AUBURN: As we mustered, we were assigned our Cabin numbers in which we were to live during our stay at Auburn.

Maybe it would be best that I describe the surroundings assigned at this Naval Training, Radio Unit. On my first impression of the grounds, I could honestly say that I never expected to live in such beautiful surroundings during my life in the U.S. Navy. There were approximately fifteen double white painted cabins set in amongst a grove of pines with a small built-in amphitheater in the center of the circle of cabins. A small macadam road ran to the end of the cabins, although it was not public thoroughfare. All this was located just at the edge of the town of Auburn. As I went to the cabin assigned me, which incidentally was (20B), I could smell the fragrant green tangy aroma of the towering pines, which were swaying gently in the breeze. Although it was only January, here in Auburn, it was perfect spring weather. At the entrance to the camp there was a small circular grass plot where the flagpole was situated.

I looked up and here was cabin 20B. Well, might as well meet the gang, I said to myself. My name is Woods! I'm Abe Combi, Junion Yiesley and so on, until I had met all twelve fellows in our side of the cabin. Another kid that made the trip down here to Auburn with us was also in the cabin. His name was Al Lowe from Holmsburg, PA, who later became one of the best pals I'd know throughout my Naval life. It wasn't hard to get acquainted at all and they were a hell of a swell bunch of fellows.

Over the weekend I took life easy as we were confined to camp and listened to what life was like, what to do and not to do. I also started to learn the phonetic alphabet and the Morse Code, which I thought might give me a head start, but as it turned out, most of the gang did the same thing. Monday finally came and my first day at school. It was raining outside as I hit the deck at five-thirty reveille. All the fellows seemed to be in a very jubilant mood at the sight of rain, which puzzled me until I found out there was no school, as long as it rained. You see, the radio school was located in town and since we would have to march about a mile in the rain, it was very unreasonable. The rain stopped early afternoon, time enough for two more classes. And so went my first day of school at Auburn. It's not so bad, I said to myself. Here, is praying for the rainy season though. As the weeks went by I made good progress and did okay in all the four subjects of typing, Naval Radio Procedure, Code and Theory.

Liberty was granted Monday, Wednesday, Friday, Saturday and Sunday nights from after school until nine o'clock at night. Auburn, however, was a very dull town. Strictly a small college town. However, the people were very nice to the Naval Personnel. The girls were very friendly, but if I may say so, dumb and silly as hell, but attractive. That was the average girl, there were exceptions though.

The liquor situation was really bad. This was a dry county and we had to go over to the nearby town of Obelika, five miles away, to get our "booze" or get a taxi driver to run over and get it for us at a price of five dollars a pint, which didn't prove very profitable for a guy making only fifty-four bucks a month, as we were. Obelika also supplied the other than nice type of girls. The bucksome, "rough and ready" variety. Mostly ready though, which explained the reason that the town had one of the highest rates of venereal disease records (based on population) in Alabama.

I spent most of my time hanging around Benson's drug store, the USO was undoubtedly the best place to make connections; women that is! A lot of college babes came up there a few nights a week to contribute their share to the war effort, I guess. I did meet some damned pretty girls. Just friendly connections though. Good after school tennis dates or something like that. Sundays we'd usually go out to Chewalka State Park for a suntan on the beach or a swim in the beautiful lake. Chewalka was a very beautiful place located about ten miles out of Auburn, back in the hills. We had many happy and memorable moments there. Al Lowe, this blond haired kid from Homesburg and I, usually traveled together. I also had my first plane ride down in Alabama. We hitchhiked to the airport one Sunday afternoon and took a fifteen-minute ride in a "Pipe Cub."

The months went by pretty fast at first. These fellows in out cabin were leaving one-by-one, as they were graduating levels ahead of us. It was tough to see good pals move along. We were getting tired of the place and wanted to get out. We wanted to get out to sea and help win the war and we didn't know how well off we actually were at Auburn, which we did realize during our later life.

They were getting more strict at camp as the days passed now. Cutting liberty, marching and exercises three nights a week after school and that made us want to get out more than ever. One Saturday afternoon we put on a marching exhibition before the review of the English Lord and Lady Halifax, which possibly highlighted my Auburn life.

I spent a few weekend passes in the capitol of Montgomery, Alabama; wine, women and song. A swell town Montgomery was. Also, I had the good fortune of seeing my brother Dick, who was stationed near Anniston, Alabama. He also came to visit me once during my stay in Auburn.

Finally came to the end of our fourth and last level term. My marks were good enough to graduate with the rating of a Third Class Radio Operator, which wasn't bad at all.

We all were excited at leaving and wondering where to next. How about this leave we were to get at the conclusion of our training down here? I had my fingers crossed anyhow. Finally, on Saturday afternoon we were called up in front of the Chief's cabin where we got our draft assignments. Some were to leave this evening already for Texas and Florida, some tomorrow morning for Philadelphia and another draft later Sunday for Norfolk, Virginia. Well, I got the Sunday afternoon draft for Norfolk. No leave connected with it either! Saying good-by to all the friends was a tough job. Especially Al Lowe and Dave Bunton from Freehold, New Jersey, who were two of my best pals at school.

I will never forget that final march through Auburn and past Benson's Drug Store to the station. As we passed Benson's, Mrs. Benson, a lady of about fifty, was waving to us. Guess she felt as though we were her own. It was the favorite hangout of all the fellows.

CHAPTER 7

Life at radio school was deluxe. After four months of radio school I graduated with a rating as Third Class Radioman. From Auburn I was shipped to Norfolk, Virginia where I spend approximately eighteen hours at an outgoing unit.

Four PM, Sunday afternoon found us (eight in our draft) headed toward Atlanta, Georgia. Atlanta to Richmond, Virginia and our last leg from Richmond to Norfolk.

Upon arrival at the receiving station Norfolk, our records were opened and I learned I was assigned to the light Cruiser "U.S.S. Boise." The Boise being a ship with quite a background to Her. I felt quite good. A ship with a memorable record of having sunk six Japanese ships in twenty minutes in the battle of Cape Esperance. The other fellow being assigned to the Cruiser Savannah. Also assigned to the Cruiser Boise were Johnny Maier of New York City and a small rebel, Jesse Abshire from West Virginia. Abshire was rated, but Maier was a seaman striker. Our first thought was to put in for a leave, which we did. However, fate again stepped in and as we were being interviewed for leaves next morning, the Boise draft was called for and off to Hampton Road where the Boise was docked was what was in store for us.

Man, I didn't know what the hell to think! All kinds of questions passed through my mind. I'd never been on a ship before in my life and I knew now that I wouldn't see home for a long time. Maybe never!

"All men for the Boise off here," shouted the truck driver. I looked up to see this big "boat" (but I soon learned to call it a ship) before me. What a big ship! Lots larger than I had expected for a Cruiser, however,

I didn't know the difference at the time. I was beginning to feel sick already. Up the gangway with my sea bag on my left shoulder. Two long years and eight months later I carried my sea bag down the same gangway for the happiest moment of my life.

We were shown around the ship and everything seemed like one big mess to me. How I wished I were down in Auburn right now. When I saw the radio shack full of radio equipment, I felt I had learned nothing at all at radio school. It was not at all as I had pictured it in my conception. About forty radio operators in all, instead of the two or three as I had expected; extremely different. The next two days the three of us spent in becoming accustomed to the layout of the ship and many times we became lost.

After maneuvers for about six weeks in the Chesapeake Bay, my journey began. Boarded the Boise approximately May 14, 1943.

Underway tomorrow, was the word I heard being passed around by the crew. Gosh! Would I get seasick? Where were we going? It was now about the middle of May 1943 and I was to get underway for the first time on one of Uncle Sam's mighty units of the fleet. Somehow I couldn't help feeling a bit proud, even though it was just a training cruise in the Chesapeake Bay. For the next month we pulled in and out for short cruises.

June 16, 1943

Finally on June 16, 1943 the scuttlebutt was that tomorrow was the day. We were getting underway for overseas and so it happened that on June 17, 1943 we pulled out of Norfolk, Virginia, destination, the Mediterranean Sea.

I recall the words as our "Captain, the abuit" spoke to us about six o'clock that night. I was in the mess hall and all hands crowded around the loud speaker system to hear what the "dope" was.

June 29, 1943

After a safe trip across the Atlantic Ocean with a convoy of approximately twenty-four merchant ships, fourteen destroyers and the light Cruiser Philadelphia and Birmingham, we arrived and passed through the straits of Gibralter on June 29. We joined up with a convoy of transports for the Mediterranean Sea.

After about ten days of alertness and changing course to dodge flocks of submarines, which the Germans had stations throughout the Atlantic, we left the rest of the convoy by a day out of Gibralter and proceeded with two destroyers for "Oran." It was evening as we passed through the straits of Gibralter and the most amazing sight was watching the porpoises swimming at unbelievable speed through the water along side of the ship. My first glimpse of foreign soil.

June 30, 1943

Pulled into "Oran" to refuel and then headed for "Algiers," the capital of Algeria in North Africa. Algiers looked like a beautiful city from the harbor. Algiers lies on the side of an immense mountain and with all its white buildings and flat-topped red roofs was a disappointment. I found out later how filthy the interior of the city actually was. We lay at anchor in the harbor in Algiers for a few weeks.

Underway in the morning for my first big invasion (two hours).

July 10, 1943

The Invasion of Sicily: The day was dreary and the fog horns were busy sounding their timely warnings as we pulled out of the ship clogged harbor. What actually was happening, I didn't know, but it didn't exactly take a war minded person to know that an invasion was not too far off, for convoy after convoy had been arriving in Algiers for the past few weeks. We anchored outside of the breakwater all day and an hour or so before sundown we got underway with the light Cruisers

Brooklyn, Philadelphia, Savannah and Birmingham. All of the same class, except the Birmingham, which was a newer type having her five inch 38 guns in shields.

These cruisers, plus destroyers were divided into two separate scouting forces to operate about twenty miles apart. In our task group was the Philadelphia and Savannah, plus destroyers.

Where or when was not known for the next few days. However, Southern France or Italy seemed to be as good a guess as Sicily.

Now this job of our scouting force was to cruise the course of the oncoming convoy and destroy our German raiders or resistance, which might be in our path.

We joined on with the mightiest invasion fleet in history (approximate 3,000 craft and ships) and landed troops at "Gela," on the southeastern coast of Sicily. Zero hour was 0200. British units landed on the southwestern coast. About the third day in the Mediterranean the Captain spoke, "now here it is," as the Captain spoke. The place is "Sicily," the spot "Gela" on the southeast coast. We pick up our landing force sometime Thursday night and land them at Gela on July 10, 1943.

This landing will take place on the same date. On Friday night a 2400 (midnight), between 1,500 and 2,000 Paratrooper Commandoes will be dropped in the vicinity of the beachhead to knock out searchlights, shore batteries and other interfering installations.

Came Thursday near sunset and we spotted the convoy, as far as the eye could see there were ships to be seen. Everything from the little PC subchasers to the large transports. What a sight! I didn't even know the Navy had half this amount. This force of 3,000 craft and ships was the largest striking force yet assembled. What a sight to review.

After joining the convoy our speed was cut to about 9 knots. The sea started getting rough on Friday afternoon and what a beating those flat-bottomed LCIS and LST's took. They looked submerged as the large waves sometimes completely covered those small craft and just stopping to think how sick those "dog faces" were was a crime. How they survived it and got into shape for the invasion in the morning is beyond me.

The sea was choppy, but everything went okay. We fired the first shot and put out a searchlight. From a few miles out you could hear the machine gun fire on the beach. Paratrooper Commandoes had landed about ten o'clock and had taken care of searchlights and shore batteries, etc. and really did a good job. Our planes were bombing Gela and the Germans really put up a barrage of "Flack."

Finally about nine o'clock that night the sea quieted down and at nine-thirty we went to General Quarters.

Midnight and we were about ten miles off shores, just laying out there until morning. Presumably, the transport planes were over the city now as the Nazi defenders were putting up a stiff barrage of anti-aircraft fire. A few searchlights were pointed out toward sea searching for the force at sea, but to no avail, as the beams went over us a few times. The German planes were also dropping flares now and a few lingered not very far from us. As I went out on the Communication Deck, just outside the radio shack, I saw all this. It looked very beautiful, although I did not appreciate this at the time. Just like the fourth of July, I said to myself. Just about now the searchlights were mighty close to getting us in their beam. So we took a bearing on the position and let go with a five-inch Salvo. The first shot we fired in the invasion of Sicily put out a searchlight position. The rest of the night the German planes had us on the alert, but caused no damage as they dropped a few bombs harmlessly around us.

Finally came the signal for the pre-invasion bombardment at approximately 0530 just before dawn. The bombardment ended at 0630 and our craft started moving in toward shores. The radio circuits were a mad house at this stage of the game.

The first wave met pretty stiff resistance, as I could hear the machine gun fire on the beach from the ship, plainly.

About 0730, as I was down in the mess hall going through the chow line, the "Jerrys" found themselves and realized what was going on and they decided to attach the fleet unit off-shores. Not a very large attack though, about fifteen planes, which we readily took care of, combined with our "air cover of P-40's. Not very much damage. A few transports took bomb hits. All day long we bombarded sporadically as the shore fire control party consisting of Army Communications men ashore radioed targets for us to bombard.

About eleven in the morning we received an urgent message calling for immediate fire as the Jerrys were throwing large scale tank attacks on our beachhead. Since this attack took place in the area, we were to cover with our guns; we received bearings and started shooting.

We started our bombardment of ammunition dumps, troops, etc. On the beach our troops had advanced inland as far as two miles at some points. In the afternoon the Nazis threw a whole division of tanks into the battle and started to give our troops a little trouble. Slow at first, but increased to fifteen gun salvos as we were finding the target. The bombardment lasted for about three-quarters of an hour. "Cease firing" was ordered. The job well done. As we found out later from Army men ashore, we had knocked out eighteen of the thirty-six attacking tanks. Some had been direct hits, which is amazing and unbelievable as we were sitting a few miles off shore. The Army men ashore later told us it was the most amazing piece of shooting they had ever seen.

It was three in the afternoon and our beachheads were well established. Advanced units had moved in four to five miles already meeting only sporadic resistance. There were fires burning ashore and the city itself was a smoking mass of ruins.

I finally secured from General Quarters about three in the afternoon after about eighteen hours of continuous watch standing coping Malta fox sheds. I went below to grab a few hours of "shuteye." I had just gotten below and layed in my "sack" when the announcement came over the public address system, as I recall, "a large scale enemy air attack is imminent." Gosh, I thought, where will I be safest, topside or down here. Anyhow, I must have fallen asleep. I woke up an hour later to the sound of five inchers and HO MIM anti-aircraft guns pounding away furiously. This must be it, I said. Everyone was rushing topside as I started doing the same. Just as I got out of my sack a large explosion occurred in the water about amid ship. I thought we had been hit, as the ship rocked from the explosion. But no, we had been lucky. We had two near misses on both port and starboard sides of the ship, about thirty feet on each side. The explosion of the thousand pound bombs had thrown water over the deck and drenched the men on the gun mounts. No one was hurt though. However, three ships were hit in the thirty-five plane attack. One big ammunition ship was burning furiously about a mile off of our starboard bow and off our port beam a large troop transport had taken a hit and the men were abandoning both ships.

Just before sundown the ammunition ship slid softly under the water after a violent explosion had split Her in two. The next two days we fired moderately on call by the shore fire control party. We had a few air raids, but no large scale and no ships were damaged. Five days after the invasion the cruisers pulled out for Algiers leaving the destroyers in charge of the operations and firing.

We had been at General Quarter since eleven o'clock Friday night until the next afternoon. We had about four air raids on Saturday and had a few close bomb misses.

July 11, 1943

Today we had our closest escape yet. About twenty-five German bombers came over and dropped one about twenty-five feet from midship. Water flew all over the starboard side of the deck (Gun seven). They dropped flares after darkness and tried to locate us, but without avail.

After hanging around Gela for about six days bombarding objectives, we set sail with the Philadelphia (42) for Algiers. Spent two weeks in Algiers and then set sail for Palermo the capital of Sicily on the northern coast. We had a few air raids there, but had no close calls.

We were following the Army up the coast towards the Straits of Messing, which are between Sicily and Southern Italy. We were out bombarding out every other day for about a week. One day while bombarding Palazzo, a shore battery opened up on us. We destroyed bridges, roads and an ammunition dump to halt the retreating Germans. Around the twelfth of August our troops marched into Messina. A few nights later we made an attack upon the mainland of Italy. The first American Warship to bombard on the mainland of Italy. The town was Palmi on the southwestern coast.

A few days later found us back in the harbor at Algiers taking on a supply of ammunition and food supplies. I went ashore a few times and we got our first mail for which we were damned glad to receive. A month and half supply approximately.

CHAPTER 8

The next few weeks saw us make a few trips between Gela and Algiers, but they were just routine trips. No excitement. General Patton's armies had advanced rapidly up the Sicilian coast and as they advanced we supplied the needed bombardment, knocking out bridges, tunnels and like installations.

While supplying bombardment, one day up on the Northern Sicilian shore near the Straits of Messina, a German shore battery opened up on us placing salvos very close spraying the ship with shrapnel. This was when our first casualty occurred. One man was killed and about five injured.

The end of the Sicilian campaign came in late August, as we were sitting in the Sicilian capital at Palermo. Messina had fallen after a two-day bloody battle, and then to Aran where we spent a few weeks.

September 3, 1943

We were called up for a special mission. As it turned out, we were to bombard a couple of electricity making plants on the mainland of Italy near Palmi. Incidentally, this made us the first American Warship to bombard the coast of Italy proper. Mission accomplished without trouble.

Italy surrendered unconditionally. We were happy for we thought the fight for Italy was practically over.

With about twenty-five troop transports and the cruisers Boise, Philadelphia (41) and Savanna (42) and a bunch of "cans," we were bound for Galerno Bay to start the invasion of Italy. On the way we made an unscheduled stop at Bizerta and there the Boise received orders to remain behind while the invasion fleet continued. The Boise with two British Battleships, about eight British cruisers and four British "can" started out for Tarento, which is located in the heel of Italy on the Southeastern coast. All the cruisers were loaded with British commandoes and motorized cavalry. We were to put these commandoes ashore at Tarento. The objective being to get these troops to the port of Tarento as quickly as possible and seize the port before the Nazis knew what was happening. We made Tarento in about a day and a half and we accepted the surrender of the Italian fleet (two battleships and a few cruiser and destroyers). They sailed out of port headed for Malta while we pulled in. We had no trouble as the reliable Boise was the first ship in. The battleship stayed out and stood by for any trouble. We worked all night to unload the troops and equipment and at 0900 next morning we got underway.

September 9, 1943

We landed at Salerno. While in the Mediterranean we saw quite a few ships sunk around us. In Gela a large ammunition ship blew up about three hundred yards from us. In Salerno about four liberty ships, two destroyers (Bristol and Rowan) and a hospital ship were sunk. In Tarento a British can was sunk as we were unloading troops on the dock.

In Algiers Harbor two tankers were blown up (sabotage) and a destroyer was destroyed by an unknown explosion.

We were bound for Bizerta, where we refueled and immediately got underway for Salerno Bay. We learned that the Savannah was hit with a rocket bomb the night of the invasion and was now in Malta.

We pulled into Salerno Bay Sunday morning on the ninth of September 1943. We had about five air raids during the day and as night was falling three Messershmits attacked our ship. They dropped about five bombs within a hundred feet of the ship, but we received no direct hits.

September 11, 1943 (Monday)

For the next four days we were under constant air attack. The Army was being driven and things looked bad. The turning point came around the eleventh of September when the Boise, plus the Philadelphia started bombarding with everything we had. We blew a couple of ammunition dumps sky high and really played hell with their troops. That was the turning point. The next morning the fifth army started their big offensive. In two more days they were practically out of range of our guns and as we pulled out of Salerno Bay the night of September fourteenth, we could see the heavy artillery of the Army flashing constantly. Our job was well done. The Navy again saved the day. We lost about seven ships in the Bay.

CHAPTER 9

September 16, 1943

Pulled into Palermo and remained in here for about three weeks. While in Palermo I ran into Uncle Woody and did we celebrate. I met him in town a few days later. I had some good times in Palermo, a place which was bombed to hell.

Our orders came through to sail for Algiers. It was a pitch-black night, the sea was calm this night as we were steaming along for Algiers. It was around midnight as we were about five miles out and in the distance we could see the air attack that was in progress at Bizerta. A great amount of anti-aircraft was being put up by our batteries on the attacking Jerry Planes. A few large fires were burning, which looked like ammunition dumps. I was getting relieved from the evening watch as the midnight watch was coming on. Suddenly one of our escorting destroyers opened up as the TBS radio equipment with the following contact. As I recall, the words were, "two enemy planes coming in at 2,000 feet, distance two miles.

Immediately upon completion of the transmission a loud and violent explosion gave the ship a terrific jolt. We took a torpedo hit, I exclaimed as I picked myself up off of the radio shack deck. However, it turned out that we took another near miss astern. One of our propelling screws on the port side was peppered pretty bad, but it was still usable, so onto Algiers, which we reached the next afternoon.

In Algiers we received orders to sail for Oran. Well, thought everyone! It's the states for the Boise. They came to this conclusion since Oran is located near Gibralter and we headed in the direction of the

States, where else could we end up? But, we found out later on! In Oran another large convoy of troop transports and cargo ships were gathered.

While our week's stay in Oran, I met Johnny Burke, a kid whom I had gone to radio school with and who was now on the Cruiser Savannah.

I remember the day well as we got underway on our next assignment. It was Sunday morning, about eleven, when it was announced "Make all preparations for getting underway." By the time I finished the Sunday turkey dinner we were pulling out of the harbor.

In Oran we lost our Communication Office and one of our radio supervisors named Giraldis, who was transferred to the states to attend V-12 school, which turned out officers. Lucky guys, I thought to myself. They will miss out on this one and what a big invasion it was to be.

About five that afternoon the Captain spoke. The destination Italy. The landing will be at Salerno Bay, which is not very far south of Naples. Now what we will meet up with we don't know, but it probably will be mostly surface attacks and planes and possibly submarines. Egads, I thought to myself, if we get out of this one unscratched and untouched, we will have to be lucky as hell.

With us were the Cruisers Savannah and Philadelphia and a convoy of large APA and AKA transports and a screen of destroyers. The Birmingham and Brooklyn had left for the States. Hell, I thought what a time to send them back. They might come in handy on this operation.

Enroute for Salerno we were scheduled to stop off at Bizerta to refuel. We did this and were on our way to join the convoy again when the Boise received a message to return to port; convoy proceed on your course. Well, says I, looks like a special mission or maybe they are sending us back to the states. The next morning we got the word that the Boise with about ten British Cruisers and two British Battlewagons. The Howe and King George, incidentally the newest British BB's, were to rush a force of Commandoes on a high-speed operation to Torento, Italy.

Since the capitulation of Italy was at hand, the allies wanted to rush troops into different parts of Italy as fast as possible before the Germans knew what was happening. Since they had to do that in a hurry, before the Nazis had a chance to reshuffle their troops, they picked on these warships to do the job.

Incidentally, the Boise was the only American representative in the group. We also were scheduled to accept the surrender of the Italian Fleet at Tarento.

The troops, which were all British Commandoes started pouring aboard. What a bunch of hardened guys they were. They had fought all through the North African Campaign. We carried about eight hundred and the decks were laden with jeeps, machine guns and even bicycles. What a sight of activity that ship was. Two and a half-hours.

October 8, 1943

We got these order sheets each day:

Excerpts from Seventh Fleet Letter A2-11(1) P7 Serial 3982, dated 8 October 1943.

Subject: Marriages of Personnel in the SEVENTH FLEET.

1. Authority to act upon marriage request of personnel of the Navy and Marine Corps in the SEVENTH FLEET is hereby delegated to:

    The Commander Submarines, SEVENTH FLEET.
    The Commander SEVENTH Amphibious Force.
    The Commander Service Force, SEVENTH FLEET.
    The Commander Aircraft, SEVENTH FLEET.
    The Commander Task Force SEVENTY-TWO.
    The Commander Destroyers, SEVENTH FLEET.
    The Commander Motor Torpedo Boat Squadrons, SEVENTH FLEET.

2. Final action upon a request to marry will be taken after a period of six (6) months from the date of the original request, unless exceptional circumstances (pregnancy) warrant a prior approval.

3. You will continue to forward to Commander SEVENTH FLEET marriage requests, which involve matters of policy, Australian relations, racial differences or extraordinary circumstances.

4. Forward report of final action in each case to the Commander Service Force, SEVENTH FLEET, in order that all marriages of personnel in this area will be recorded in one office.

J. CARY JONES,
Deputy

CHAPTER 10

October 10, 1943

Around the tenth of October we sailed for Algiers and spend about seventeen days there. Made some good liberties. The best one being on the "Chaplains Wine Party." The afternoon beach party, which was organized by the Chaplain of the ship, and what a party that turned out to be. We bought a couple barrels of good wine and rolled it out on the beach. Everyone got drunk as hell and the Chaplain himself took quite a beating as he was thrown in the water, clothes and all! We got a good poker game going, which our chief radioman Wang Ju and myself cleaned up. We came out a couple hundred dollars on top. It was sunset as we started back to the ship. Everyone stinken drunk, but happy as hell.

Next it was Oran and ten days in Casablanca.

hou. 1943 - PA.

NOVEMBER 1943 PA.

CHALMERS H. HALLMAN

RADIOMAN RM 3/C

CHAPTER II

November 8, 1943

On November the eighth we pulled from Casablanca headed for the Brooklyn Navy Yard, New York and what a happy bunch we were. I now look forward to my first leave since joining the Navy a year ago.

With two destroyers, the Rhind and Nichleson, we pulled into Sheepsend Bay after a seven-day trip over the wild Atlantic. We sprung a leak coming across and had about three feet of water in one of the compartments.

November 15, 1943

After a hard day unloading all the ammunition from the ship and preparing Her for dry-dock, we round out the first leave party was to leave the ship the same night. I had the first party and after rushing around in an excited daze I left the ship at about eight-thirty for an eight-day leave. Took a taxi for Penn Station and got a train at 11:45 PM. Arrived in Allentown about 0230 AM. Got a lift home and got the folks out of bed about 0330, and what a happy family we were.

Spent a wonderful eight days at home and four liberties in New York. Met Marge Cartagena, what a gal!

NOVEMBER 1943 PA

MY PARENTS

PERCY AND SADIE HALLMAN

AND CHALMERS

CHAPTER 12

December 3, 1943

Did not waste anytime getting us out of the Navy Yard. On the fifth of December we sailed for Panama. Had a rough sea the first few days, but after we hit the Caribbean Sea the water was smooth.

December 9, 1943

Passed through the Panama Canal, about six locks.

December 10, 1943

Spent one day and two nights in Balboa. Liberty for second class and above.

December 12, 1943

Underway—destination Bora Bora. Approximately 4,100 miles, ten days traveling. Boise traveled alone.

December 22, 1943

Arrived in Bora Bora, a beautiful island. Refueled. About fifty canoes came out to meet the ship to sell souvenirs. Underway the same day for Suva in the Fiji Islands. 1,500 miles Boise traveling alone.

December 24, 1943

Crossed the International Date Line and gained a day, so officially we had only about five hours of Christmas.

December 26, 1943

Had our Christmas meal on the high seas. It was really a swell meal. Turkey, ice cream, pie, olives, pickles, gravy, potatoes, peas, candy, nuts, cigarettes, cigars and all the other trimmings.

Arrived in Suva around 1500. Refueled the ship. Liberty from 1800 to 2200. I did not rate liberty. Have not been ashore since New York.

December 27, 1943

Underway for Milne Bay on New Guinea. Weather is torrid.

December 29, 1943

Entered Milne Bay.

December 31, 1943

Left Milne Bay for Buna Roads. Joined the Cruisers Nashville (43) and Phoenix (46). Anchored at Porloch Bay. We are in Crudiv 15 T.F.74.7th Fleet. We made daily trips between Buna Roads and Porloch Bay.

January 14, 1944

Back to Milne Bay: Joined up with the Aussie Cruiser Shropshire. Nashville Cruiser went to Sydney, Australia for a rest.

January 20, 1944

Went ashore for the first time since November 30th in New York. Had a beer party on the beach and had an enjoyable time. Almost missed the last boat back to the ship.

January 25, 1944

This is it. Our first action in the Southwest Pacific. Underway at 12:30 for Buna Roads.

January 26, 1944

Left Buna Roads at 12:30. The plan was for the Boise and one destroyer to attack and bombard installations at Alexshafen and the Phoenix and two destroyers to attack eight miles south of Alexshafen at Madang. We sailed into the bay at Alexshafen at 0115 on schedule and due to some foul-up we did not start our bombardment until 0150. We put out around 500 rounds of five inch and 600 rounds of six inch. We were not very effective though, as there was a foul-up in taking a bearing on the target. The Phoenix did all right though. We had a "PBY" spotting for us. Our destroyer the Mullany scored quite a few hits and started several fires. We sailed away at 29 knots. Japs opened up with shore batteries and wounded three of our men. No direct hit, just shrapnel wounds.

January 27, 1944

Anchored in Porlock Bay the next day.

January 28, 1944

Left Porlock Bay for Milne Bay.

January 29, 1944

Still hanging around Milne Bay, Nashville rejoined us.

January 30, 1944

Went ashore for the third time in New Guinea. Had a few quarts of ale.

February 1, 1944

Underway at 0730. Went into the outer harbor of Milne Bay for AA practice and returned to Milne Bay at 1600. Received word of the invasion of the Marshall Islands.

February 2, 1944

It rains every day now, probably is their rainy season. Was going ashore today, but it rained too hard. The move was postponed. I got a few Christmas greetings and a v-mail letter from home and one from Connie.

February 3, 1944

It rained practically all day. Sat in a drizzling rain to see the picture "Bill the Kid" with Robert Taylor. It was a swell show.

February 4, 1944

Held field day this morning. I had the watch this afternoon and I have the 12 to 0800 midnight watch tonight. "Arsenic and Old Lace" is playing tonight. I think I shall see it.

February 5, 1944

Had Captain's inspection this morning. After inspection I crapped out until five this afternoon. Missed noon chow. Movie postponed tonight. Had dressing changed on my ingrown toenail. It hurts like hell.

CHAPTER 13

February 6, 1944

Wrote a few letters, but slept most of the day. Had the evening watch, but was relieved so I could go to the movies. It was a rotten show. Name of the picture was "Chatterbox."

February 7, 1944

Saw Mickey Rooney in "Andy Hardy's Private Secretary." Sat in a driving rain for about an hour to see the show.

February 9, 1944

Had fire drills, etc. this afternoon. It's pretty much of a pain in the ass.

February 10, 1944

Had drills in the afternoon. Had the evening watch. The Admiral of COM CRU Division 15 came aboard the Boise as the "Flag" is coming aboard and the Phoenix is going to Australia for a rest.

February 11, 1944

Had field day and the afternoon watch.

February 12, 1944

It was raining practically all day. I had charge of the drill circuit on 805 KC's this afternoon.

February 14, 1944

Nothing exciting going on. Saw the movie this evening. Name of it was "Are Husbands Necessary." A terrible show.

February 15, 16, 17, 18, 19, 1944

No comments.

February 20, 1944

Has the morning watch. Has a happy hour on the fantail. A couple of nurses from the beach attended (a red head and a blond). The fellows just about went crazy. Had a few boxing matches and they were pretty good. After the happy hour they served punch, cake and handed out cigars, cigarettes and candy. After that they showed a swell movie, "Gentlemen After Dark." Starring Brian Donlevy and Mirian Hopkins. Slept topside and really had a good night's sleep.

February 21, 1944

Today, or rather this morning, I washed my blues and am getting them in shape for I am expecting to get liberty in Australia in the near future. It's about 1115 now and I have to relieve the watch as I have got the afternoon watch.

CHAPTER 14

February 25, 1944

Underway at 6:30 AM this Friday morning. It's a beautiful morning as we sailed out of Milne Bay for the Pacific. Most of the men were topside to get a good look at scenery, which is very picturesque on each side of the Bay. The Bay is quite long and it takes about an hour and a half to the Ocean. Many small islands are scattered throughout it. With us were the Shropshire, Nashville and five Cans (destroyers), the Boise and a Submarine. Our objective was to have exercises with the Sub, periscope spotting, torpedo dodging, etc., and also a practice surface battle. This all took place in the Coral Sea. Had drill General Quarters at 2000. It lasted until 2230. I had the 12 to 0700 watch coming up.

February 26, 1944

Pretty sleepy throughout the mid-watch. At 0630 we separated from the rest of the task force and on our own started for Sydney, Australia. Hope for a little good liberty there. Tonight I finally pressed my blues. I am all set now. Think I will hit the "sack" now, although I did sleep all day.

February 27, 1944

We got these order sheets each day.

U.S.S. BOISE

27 February 1944

ORDERS FOR THE DAY—MONDAY, 28 FEBRUARY 1944

DUTY HEAD OF DEPARTMENT   Comdr. Cassidy
DUTY SECTION: 1st
DUTY DIVISION: 6th

UNIFORM OF THE DAY—OFFICERS & COP'S: Khaki without ties.
                           ENLISTED MEN: Dungarees without shirts,
                                      blue hats, (carry shirts).

0000	-	Execute ship's routine with the following substitutions and additions.
0505	-	All hands.
0535	-	Precautionary General Quarters.
0635	-	Sunrise. Light ship. Secure from G.Q.
0830	-	Quarters for muster and physical drill, except Engineers.
0900	-	Division officers inspect lockers and bedding. Check blue dress uniforms of division.
1100	-	Quarters for Engineers.
1230	-	Pay Day for officers in wardroom.
1430	-	Physical drill for Officers Cooks and St Mates.
1700	-	All division check condition settings and make report to the D.C. office.
1900	-	Hammocks.

NOTES: 1. Water consumed for the previous 24 hours was 18.9 gallons per man.
            2. Anyone knowing the whereabouts of sheepskin coat #5 please notify or turn in to the Damage Control Office.
            3. All mess cooks report to HUNNEWELL, SClc, in the Issuing Room at 0800.

4. 1 hand each from the first four deck divisions report to STILES, CCS, in the Issuing Room at 0800.

5. 1 hand from each deck division and 2 hands from the Engineering divisions report to HINZE, SK2c, in the Supply Office at 0800.

6. All men interested in designing special occasion and holiday cards (to be mimeographed on V-mail letter forms) report to Lt. Balis in the Optical Shop at 0915 today.

7. The rate between the U.S. dollar and Australian pound is fixed at $3.228 per pound. The denominations of Australian money are pounds, shillings and pence.

1 pound	$3.228	10 pound notes	$32.28
20 shillings	1 (pound)	5 pound notes	16.14
12 pence (d)	1 (shilling)	1 pound note	3.23
2 shillings	1 (florin)	10 shillings note	1.61
		1 florin (coin)	.32
Prices of goods are written:		1 shilling (coin)	.16
		1 pence or penny	.01
		1/8 pence or penny	.005
s d		6 pence (coin)	.08
5/12/11		3 pence (coin)	.04

8. As everyone knows, a high percentage of sexually promiscuous women are infected with venereal disease. Also, we all know, there are certain men who will have sexual intercourse with these women. Some of them do so intentionally; others became exposed while under the influence of too much to drink. To lessen the incidence of venereal disease and safeguard our health, there are certain protective measures available to all who so expose themselves. The measure of greatest importance is use of a condom. These are on sale at the Ship's Service Store. The condom must be put on before either the hands or penis become exposed to infection.

After completing intercourse the condom should be removed carefully in order that the outer side does not come in contact with the penis. Infection may also develop if infected material becomes smeared on the skin of the thighs adjacent to the genitals. Immediately after exposure, one should urinate to cleanse out the urethra. Then wash exposed parts thoroughly preferably with soap and water. This should be followed (as soon as possible and preferably within one or two hours) by the injection of protargol solution into the penis (hold solution in penis for 5 minutes), and then thoroughly massage contents of sanitube (obtain in Sick Bay) into all exposed areas.

T. M. WOLVERTON
Cmdr., U.S. Navy
Executive Officer.

February 29, 1944

This morning at 0830 we docked at Wallamalu Landing, Pier #9 at Sydney. The harbor of Sydney is very beautiful. I went ashore at 1100 AM. The first thing I did was take my watch to the jewelers for repair. We ate chow at a very exclusive restaurant. After chow we met up with a couple of girls. Dated them up for 1930. Having the afternoon all to ourselves, my pal and I started hitting the bars. By 1600 we were pretty well under. Not able to walk so damn straight; we went looking for a room, but to no avail. We did find one room though, although it was dirty as hell. Cost us a pound. Frankly speaking though, it was the same as a "Cat House." After spending about five minutes in our room we were visited by a couple of beautiful blonds (their price 10 pounds). Being the fellow I am and as fussy as I am, I kicked them out and rang for the landlady. She came and I told here I demanded a refund, that we decided not to keep the room. I gave her a pretty good talking to and I was pretty mad. She finally gave us our two pounds back and told us to get the hell out. We ate chow and by 1930 we were sobered up and met our dates at the Ferry landing. My date was about five feet two inches and very cute and also respectable. Nice kid. Took in a show and had a good time. Kissed her in the picture. I think she took to me. At 2300 we caught a ferry and took them home. After catching a ferry back to Sydney we met a couple of "pick ups" and started out again. All places close up at 0200, so there wasn't much to do except "bum" around town. We finally hit the subway and my girl had to wait until 0500 for a train. Three hours to wait, so we parked on a bench in the subway. I could do anything with her I liked. She finally fell asleep in my arms and after a half-hour of consideration I figured, hell this isn't worth missing some good sleep. She had wanted me to go home with her. So I slipped away and left her. Got back aboard ship around 0300 and slept until 0830.

March 1, 1944

Rated liberty again today, so I went ashore at 1000. After just bumming around town most of the morning we went into a theatre at 1330 and slept through a couple shows. 1730 we were bound for Luna Park. At the park we picked up two very respectable girls. Mine was very young (18) and very beautiful. She looked very much like Diana Durbean. Rode about all the amusement rides, including the Roller Coaster about four times straight and I just about had to drag her off of it. Sweet kid. We left the park at 2200. Took a ferry back to Sydney and then took the girls home. They lived on the out-skirts of Sydney. My girl's name was Betty Mulligan. We spent the remainder of the time until 0100 on a park bench and had an enjoyable time. Left them and headed back for the ship. Got a taxi back part way and walked the rest of the way. Dated Betty up for 1915 coming Friday night. By the way, this makes two dates for Friday night, one with Patricia at 1730 and Betty at 1916. Don't know which to take. Both very pretty. Time will tell.

March 2, 1944

Have the duty today. Slept until 0830 and went on watch at 0930. Just finished eating chow as I am bringing this diary up-to-date.

March 3, 1944

Met Betty at 1900. Got off the ship about 1100 and went with Kelm, Grieco, Perkins and Kniep up to Griecos Shack. Decided to go horse-back riding so we took a train to a place called Pymble, about 18 miles outside of Sydney. I got an old nag and had one hell of a time with it.

"A SAILOR'S LIFE"

'A SAILORS LIFE IS A JOLLY LIFE.
AS THEY SAY IN THE OLD NAY-V.
BUT WE'RE GETTING TIRED OF THE STRESS AND STRIFE
AND CONDITION ONE E-Z.
AND THE NIPPON VALS AND BETS SO RIFE
IN THE GULF OF OLD LAY-T.
IF YOU DIAGREE JUST ASK HIS WIFE;
OR HIS GAL IN TENNA-C.

THE LOOKOUT STRAINS IN THE SUN'S BRIGHT GLARE
TILL HIS EYES FEEL ALMOST DEAD.
THEN HE STAGGERS OFF WITH A GLASSY STARE
AND THE THOUGHTS RUN TROUGH HIS HEAD
OF ONE AT HOME WHO HAS NO CARE
ASLEEP IN A SOFT WHITE BED.
THE BUGLE BLOWS AND YOU HEAR HIM SWEAR
FLASH WHITE! FLASH BLUE! FLASH RED!

THEN IT'S GRAB A LINE AND HAUL LIKE HELL
THEN TAKE A REST AND BLOW;
TOTE THAT POWDER; THEN GRAB A SHELL

AND STRIKE IT DOWN BELOW
LASHIT DOWN IN PLACE AND STOW IT WELL
FOR WHO CAN SAY OR KNOW
WHICH ONE OF THESE WILL DOWN A NELL
ON THE ROAD TO TOKYO.

IT'S 'COMMANDER THIS' AND 'COMMANDER THAT'
":WHEN CAN WE FEED THE CREW?"
"WHERE IN THE HELL IS THE BLANK BLANK <u>CAP</u>?"
CONDITION THREE—WATCH TWO!
HEAVE AROUND, THEN TRY TO CATCH A NAP
COMES THE BUGLE CALL TO YOU
TO DEFEND THE SHIP AGAINST THE JAP
FLASH RED! FLASH WHITE! FLASH BLUE!

CIC WHAT IS THE COURSE?
RANGE AND BEARING TO THE GUIDE!
WHAT'S THE DISPOSITION OF THAT FORCE?
HOW'S THE CURRENT? WHAT'S THE TIDE?
AIR PLOT, SNAP TO! GET ON YOUR HORSE!
IS THAT BOMBER IN A GLIDE?
LAUGH IT OFF! CHEER UP! HAVE NO REMORSE!
POINT MOLLY'S ON OUR SIDE.

WHEN AT THE END OF DAYS SO DREAR
I LAY ME DOWN TO SLEEP AT NIGHT
WITH THOUGHTS OF KEGS OF ICE-COLD BEER
AND STEAK COOKED RARE AND SERVED JUST RIGHT
I'LL DREAM THE END OF WAR IS HERE
AND IN THE WORLD OF NEW FOUND LIGHT
THESE WORDS I HOPE I NEVER HEAR
FLASH RED! FLASH BLUE! FLASH WHITE!

U.S. Navy
Enlisted Men's Liquor Club
64 Macleay Street, King's Cross
Honorary Membership
Not Transferable

Issued .... Expires ....

Name _____ Rank _____ Activity

Manager

U.S. Navy
Enlisted Men's Liquor Club
151 Darlinghurst Road, King's Cross
Honorary Membership
Not Transferable

Issued .... Expires ....

Name _____ Rank _____ Activity

Manager

SEE YOUR
PHOTOGRAPH
AT

Shop No. 9

VICTORIA ARCADE

3 doors from Prince Edward Theatre
Castlereagh Street

OPPOSITE

Hotel Australia

If ordering by Post, remit Postal Note
and 2¼d Stamp for Amount Required,
giving Full Description.

1 Photo 2/-

Hours of Business:
8.30 a.m. to 6 p.m.
Call and see your Proof any time after
12 noon to-morrow.

B 184 11

SHIP'S DANCE

MONDAY, MARCH 6th, 1944

AT

GRACE AUDITORIUM

Broadway and Bay Street

SYDNEY ..... AUSTRALIA

1945 - 2345

U.S.S. BOISE

Ship's Dance

TUESDAY, AUGUST 15th, 1944

GRACE BROS. AUDITORIUM

7:30 p.m. — 11:30 p.m.

COUPLES ONLY

BEARER MUST NOT
DETACH COUPONS

COUPON	COUPON
1 BOTTLE	1 BOTTLE
BEER	BEER

Old Kniep had never ridden horseback and he damn near fell off his horse. We rode for about three hours and started back. We got a lift in a truck all the way back to Sydney. We hit the Mayfair lounge for a couple drinks and Kelm and myself had chow at Clairiges. There we met Charles Perkins and his girl friends. Met Betty Mulligan at 1900 on Battleship Corner. So known because of the sailors hanging out there. Took in a show at the Plaza "Hangmen Also Die" with Brian Donley. Pretty good show. Had a milk shake after the show and then took a train to Glebe Point where she lives. Got in a couple hours of "smuching" and got back to the ship at 0230.

March 4, 1944

Got off the ship at about 1215. Ate noon chow on ship. Hung around the ferry landing until about 1330 and then met Bette at 1400. We spent the afternoon at the Zoo. Came back to Sydney for dinner at Clairiges. Took in a show "Yankee Doodle Dandy." Got out of the show at 1945 and decided to catch a steamer for a little harbor cruise. Caught the steamer at 2015. Night was quite cool, but a lovely moon was out. Had a seat out on the deck under the moonlight sky. Had a lovely time on the cruise, got back to Sydney at 2245. Stopped in for a couple sandwiches and then took Bette to her home. Got in a little more loving and got back to the ship at 0245.

March 5, 1944

Did not rate liberty today. Had a wonderful chow chicken. Had the afternoon watch and washed my blues. Pressed them in the afternoon.

March 6, 1944

Got ashore about 1045 and decided to go out to Manly Beach swimming. Thought I might as well have a few drinks before going out. I had a couple all right. Drank about twenty scotches with a couple of soldiers and got plastered as hell. At 1730 I woke up in Hyde Park. Don't know how the devil I got there. Had a date with Betty at 1845, so I had to spruce up a bit. I got a little food in my stomach and I felt better. Met Betty and then took in a show at Trwoli. Turned out to be a wonderful stage show. Had a milk shake after the show and took her home. A little loving and I got back to the ship about 0200.

March 7, 1944

Went ashore at 1015 with Petrie (Worcester). Decided to go swimming, so we took the Manly Ferry. Saw a beautiful blond on the Ferry, but we didn't attempt any passes. After renting suits and towels we hit the beach. Manly turned out to be a beautiful town. The streets were lined with palms and very clean looking. The beach was wonderful. I spotted this blond I saw on the Ferry and WOW, what a joy. Petrie was in swimming and I walked up to the blond and started talking to her. She was very accommodating and after a half-hour of conversation Petrie rejoined me.

After a while her mother joined us and we had a wonderful conversation. They had their lunch there, so they invited us to some of it. Blond's name was Jean Hall. After sandwiches we had a drink of pineapple. Finally we hit the water and had a lot of fun. The surf was nice. About four her mother left and left Jean in our custody. About five we headed back for Sydney. Took her to dinner at the Hotel Australia. Pretty ritzy joint. I had a date with Betty at 1845, so as much as I hated to do it, I turned Jean over to Petrie and told her I had another engagement. I dated her for Thursday afternoon. Planned to go riding in the afternoon. Met Betty at 1915. She wanted to go out to Manly, so I took her. The night was beautiful and the moon just about full. What a night for romance. Ocean was beautiful at night, we sat on the boardwalk for about two and half-hours. The boardwalk was full of couples and every turn of the head you could see someone loving it up. Got back to Sydney 2315 and then took her home. She and I are very close and really made progress since I met her. Have a date for Thursday, which probably will be my last night in Sydney. Pretty tough to leave her tonight.

March 8, 1944

Duty today and I felt like hell. Just had a couple hours sleep. Five gallons of alcohol was stolen from "sick bay" so they held up liberty. Finally decided to give liberty at 1300. I slept all afternoon. Ate chow and decided to catch up on my diary, so here I am. Just finished smoking a "White Owl" cigar and still tired and have a head cold. Want to be in good shape for liberty tomorrow, so I'm turning in now.

March 9, 1944

Got ashore about 1015 this morning. First thing I did was get a "shack" up at Kings Cross. Got a pretty nice room for ten shillings. Did a little shopping in the afternoon and then came back to my room and slept for about three hours. It rained most of the day and it kinda spoiled my plans for I did have a dinner date and afternoon riding date with Jean. The blond I met at Manly. I ate chow at the coffee shop at about 1800 and met Betty at 1915. It was raining slightly, so we decided on a show. We saw "Slightly Dangerous" with Lana Turner and "Talk of the Town" with Frank Morgan at the St. James. Very nice theatre. Raining pretty hard after the show, so we caught a train for Glebe Point.

I was almost positive this was my last night ashore in Sydney. It was pretty hard saying good-bye to Betty and I must say, she didn't take my leaving any too easy. After a few tears on her part we said not good-by, but so long and she promised to write every week. I felt a little sick leaving her. The seven times I had been out with her had made us the best of friends. I got back to my room around two A.M.

March 10, 1944

Got up at seven fifteen and after taking a cold shower had breakfast with Grieco, Bargetzi and Howard. Got back to the ship at 0830 and to my amazement I found out we again had liberty today. This was our last day in Sydney though, definitely. I took a shower and went off the ship at 1015 with Petrie. The day was very cool, but anyway, we decided to go out to Manly. I figured after the good-bye with Betty last night I couldn't do it again, so I called up Patricia Sherritt, same babe I dated on my first liberty (B-3873). We hit Manly at about 1200 and the beach wasn't too crowded. The sun was hot though and I spent all the day in it. Petrie and I met some little brunette and he dated her for the night. At 1630 we called it quits and he was supposed to meet her outside the bathing house, but she never showed up after we waited for about three-quarters of an hour. We went back to Sydney and had a swell chicken dinner at the coffee shop. I just made my date at 1930 by a few minutes. We took in a show at the Regent Theater "Mr. Lucky" starring Cary Grant. Swell theater and swell show. Had a shake after the show and then caught a train and then a ferry for Mosman, a suburb of Sydney. After a little loving I shoved off and said good-bye to Patricia. She promised to write. Caught a train for Wyneyard station. Got back to the ship about two and sat up in the radio shack and shot the breeze until 0300 and then retired. We were shoving off the next day.

March 11, 1944

Slept until 0800 and missed morning chow. We finally shoved off at 1030 and what a sad day for the Boise crew. They had made many good friends in Sydney. Many of the girls had come down to the waterfront to wave good-bye to the boys they probably would never see again. They were watching as long as the Boise was in sight. I ate chow and then slept all afternoon. I had the evening watch. That's all for today. The question is will we hit Sydney again??????

CHAPTER 15

March 12, 1944

Had the morning watch. We had firing practice at 1630. It is about 1942 right now and I think I will retire and think about the good times I had back in Sydney, "Finis."

March 15, 1944

We arrived at Milne Bay the morning of March fifteenth around 0830. I had the evening watch and missed the evening movie.

March 16, 1944

Morning watch. Saw the movie in the evening "It Ain't Hay."

March 20, 1944

Went ashore for a few hours. Had the morning watch. I had a few bottles of beer on the beach. They are issuing coupons to us worth two bottles of beer per week. Saw the movie at night, Henry Fonda and Barbara Stanwyk in "I Belong to You."

March 21, 1944

Underway at 0700 for exercises in the outer harbor. Gunnery practice and also towed the Australia. Had the third watch.

March 22, 1944

Slept all day. It is raining tonight, although I am hoping it stops for the movies.

March 24, 1944

Had the morning watch. In the afternoon I went ashore with the second recreation party. I had a couple of bottles of beer. Came back to the ship and about 1445 and had chow and took a shower and here I am writing these few lines. So long for today.

March 25, 1944

Slept about all day. Had a happy hour on the fantail tonight. There were about eight boxing bouts, which were good, Steve Beloise contender for the middleweight championship of the world was on board to give a boxing exhibition. After the bouts there was a movie. That was until the movie machine broke down and it was postponed. Slept topside and it was really a very cool night. So long C. H.

April 10 1944

Still hanging around Milne Bay and have been inactive the past few weeks with the exception of a few days in the Coral Sea and the outer Milne Bay area practicing shore bombardment, which incidentally didn't turn out too well. Today I received my first letters from Australia and was very happy to get them. One from Betty Mulligan and one from Patricia Sherritt. A few days ago I heard from David Bunton a pal of mine from radio school who is at present on the light Cruiser U.S.S. Santa Fe and formerly on the U.S.S. Brooklyn. According to reports, we are moving out of the Milne Bay area for good within the next week or so and in my estimation I think we might invade the area of New Guinea around Wewak or possibly at Eabaul in New Britain. Time will tell though, there are quite a few troop transports in the harbor at present. That's all for now.

April 15, 1944

We got underway at 0530. We arrived at Buna somewhere around 1600. Plenty of warships in the harbor here. Approximately forty-five destroyers, five Cruisers and quite a few patrol craft.

April 16, 1944

Got underway at 0600 and fired about thirty round of five inch and then came back in.

April 18, 1944

Slept until about 0815 today and missed chow. Had no quarters today as it was raining. We got the "dope" on what our next operation is composed of. Here it is straight from one Mr. Wangnes, a coding officer. The Cruisers Boise, Phoenix and Nashville and the Cans in task force "75," combined with Shropshire and Australia and the destroyers in task force "74" and our invasion transports are going to make a landing on the northern coast of New Guinea above the major Japanese base of Madang at the base called Hollinda. There are to be fifteen aircraft carriers to stand by in our area. We are scheduled to start our bombardment at 0615 and bombard for approximately a half an hour. After this 150 of our bombers are scheduled to come over and pour tons of bombs on the airfields and other installation, which we failed to destroy. After this our troops will be put ashore. We are due to stay around there for approximately a day. This landing will trap about 75,000 Japanese troops between Hollinda and Madan and we expect the three battleships and a few carriers, which the Japanese have in Singapore harbor to come out and try to assist in getting some of the trapped troops out of the New Guinea area. For this reason the fifth fleet composed of all the real fighting power battleships, approximately thirty carriers and many heavy cruisers, is standing by in the Gilbert Islands and the area. In other words, our action is used as a decoy to draw this portion of the Jap fleet out to fight. Here is hoping we get a crack at them. Time will tell. Invasion scheduled for twenty-second of April. So long.

April 19, 1944

Almost forgot, we got underway this afternoon at 1400. The Boise and Phoenix and five destroyers. Where we will pick the troop transports and task force "74," remains to be seen. We also left the Nashville behind in Buna, but there are rumors that she is following us. We have still got about five days before we attack though.

April 20, 1944

We are still out at sea and last night we picked up part of the invasion fleet. As the day is passing by we are gradually increasing the size of the force and as it is right now about 1600, our force consists of eight Carriers (all converted), two light and two heavy Cruisers. Approximately thirty-five destroyers and approximately somewhere between eighty and one hundred troop carrying ships. LSTL and big transports. I've been sleeping all day and have the five-to-twelve watch.

April 21, 1944

Well, this is the last notation in my diary until after the battle. I just got off the afternoon watch and don't know exactly what time we'll go to "General Quarters" tonight, but I calculate about 0100. Everything has gone smooth so far, so until my next entry, here is to a successful landing. C.H.

April 22, 1944

It's about 200 and I am pretty tired. We had quite a busy day. We went to General Quarters at 0430. We moved into the Bay at Hollandia at 0600 and started our Naval bombardment. The first invasion troops hit the beach about 0700 and met very little opposition. We started many

large fires ashore. I was at General Quarters until 1330. We got underway at 1600 and are now on our way for a base in the Admiralty Islands.
The Nashville left around noon and reports say that General MacArthur
was aboard to view the landings and bombardment. Reports are that
casualties are extremely light.

CHAPTER 16

April 23 & 24, 1944

Arrived at Manus Island, the main island in the Admiralty Islands. We hit the bay (See-Adler Bay) at approximately 1300. Manus or rather See-Adler harbor is a beautiful harbor. The entrance to the harbor is very small with coral reefs surrounding most of the harbor. Had movies on the fantail tonight, but I had the evening watch. I missed noon chow. Slept from eight-thirty until 1600.

April 24, 1944

Still at Manus Island in the Admiralties. Movies tonight. Afternoon watch.

April 26, 1944

We got underway at 0600 with a force of three light Cruisers 43, 46 and 47, four Aircraft Carriers (converted small ones) and twelve Tin Cans. As we pulled out of See-Adler Harbor the Indiana, one of our New Battlewagons, pulled in. Where we are underway for, no one knows.

April 27, 1944

We had General Quarter today at two in the afternoon and stayed at General Quarters until about 2000. We are now in the Hollandia area. Just patrolling up and down the coast in case the Japs get any ideas of evacuating some of their troops trapped between Mandang and Hollandia. We now have control of two of the Airdromes in the

Hollandia sector. About twenty-five miles inland. Twelve torpedo bombers attacked an American destroyer in this sector yesterday and that is the reason for our General Quarters.

April 28, 1944

Still cruising the waters in the Hollandia area.

April 29, 1944

Tonight we are scheduled to bombard some island north of the Hollandia area. I think our objective will be an airfield, so we might have a little excitement. More news about our activities after tonight.

April 30, 1944

Last night we bombarded Wakde Island and the mainland about one hundred twenty miles above Hollandia. It was one of the most effective jobs of bombarding I have ever seen. Large fires and explosions were started on the beach and smoke completely covered the island and made it invisible from the air, as we were told by the PBY's that spotted for us.

We started the bombarding shortly after midnight. The bombarding force consisted of the Cruisers Nashville 43, Phoenix 46, Boise 47 and six destroyers. The rest of our six destroyers were left at sea to guard the four "baby carriers."

We expended approximately eight hundred rounds of five inch and three hundred round of six inch.

Reconnaissance planes off our carriers took photos of the airstrips we bombarded and they showed that they were completely unservice-able. As we headed for sea at about two thirty AM large fires were burning fiercely. I finally hit the sack at 0330 after a little snack of sandwiches.

May 1 and 2, 1944

Still cruising between Hollandia and north and south of the island.

May 3, 1944

We pulled into Manus Island around noon today.

May 9 thru 13, 1944

I went ashore today on the recreation party. We went to a small island given to the Navy by the Army. I had two quarts of ice cold beer and it really tasted good. We went swimming in the nude and had one hell of a good time. The water is crystal clean and the beach is pretty nice. Got one hell of a suntan also.

May 15, 1944

Expect to get underway today at 1430. Destination undoubtedly somewhere in the northern section of Dutch New Guinea. I think we have got another little operation ahead of us. Time will tell.

May 17, 1944

Starting bombarding Wakde Island and the mainland of Dutch New Guinea at 0600 this morning and blasted the hell out of the place for forty minutes. Main battery six inch doing most of the firing. The first troops hit the beach at approximately 0710. Landed about 6,000 troops. Fired approximately 400 rounds of five-inch and six-inch. Our P-40's did quite a bit of dive bombing and strafing and the destroyers stood in close and really poured lead into the beach.

We left for Hollandia about 1330. Reached Hollandia about 0700 same day.

May 18, 1944

I crapped out all morning, I was exhausted. Quite a few explosions occurred on the beach this afternoon.

We learned that some old Jap ammunition fuel dumps had blown up due to carelessness of our men. Four men killed and six wounded. Fires started about 1500 and by sunset about a mile long strip along the beach was on fire. Due to the danger of air raid and with visibility good, due to the fire which incidentally lit up the whole bay, we got underway for sea.

Came back the next morning and the fires on the beach were under control

May 19, 1944

We got underway tonight at 0700. From the dope that was put out, we are making another landing, Biak Island, almost on top of Dutch New Guinea. I think this may be the last landing made to round out the New Guinea Campaign. The dope is that the landing will be made in approximately six days, which will make it the coming Saturday.

May 22, 1944

During the past few days we have been patrolling the Coast of Dutch New Guinea with an air coverage of P40's and "38's most of the time. One of the P40's crashed this morning, although the pilot bailed out and was picked up by one of the destroyers. It's about 1900 now, so I think I'll retire, as I have the mid-watch coming up. Cheerio!!!

May 23, 1944

Pulled into Hollandia this morning at 1100. Took on stores tonight, but I got out of it though.

May 25, 1944

Getting underway tonight 2100. Invasion taking place Saturday morning at Schouten Islands.

CHAPTER 17

May 26, 1944

We pulled out of Hollandia last night with our invasion force of LCI's, LST's and LCM's. Five cruisers. Quite a few Cans. Making about six knots all last night and today. We went on a two-section watch last night and are standing four hours on and four hours off. Write more after the invasion.

May 27, 1944

Started our pre-invasion bombardment of Biak Island in the Schouten Island on northwestern port of Dutch New Guinea in Geelvich Bay. After a half-hour of steady bombardment the first waves went ashore and did not encounter too much resistance. Landed about 8,000 troops all totaled. They had quite a number of shore batteries located at pretty well fortified spots. Two six inch guns, four five inch and three three-inch guns.

They scored two hits on one of our destroyers the Hutchins, the first salvo knocking off her mast and radar and the second one going clear through the hull on both sides. We kept up a periodical bombardment for the rest of the day. In the afternoon, around 1600 we were attacked by bombers. One of the destroyers, the Sampson knocked down four when she was attacked by them. In the morning our secondary batteries were firing at barges. At 1800 task force 74 pulled out for Hollandia and the Nashville was shifted to T.F-74 for the time being. That's all for now.

May 28, 29, 30, 1944

Patrolling area around Biak Island in case of enemy warships interfering.

June 3, 1944

Got underway tonight about 2345 with about 22 Cans and Nashville, Phoenix, Boise and Aussie Cruiser, Australia.

Objective is going to be a Jap task force hanging in some bay above Biak Island.

June 4, 1944

Tonight we had our first real air attack since coming out in the Pacific. About eight to ten Jap dive-bombers attacked us about 1800. The Nashville got a hole in her starboard side. One compartment is flooded. Casualties not known. The Phoenix had a couple near misses also. Six men injured on the Phoenix from shrapnel. I watched the attack from the Com-deck. Boy what a sight. Think they will probably be back. Tonight a surface battle is imminent. Don't know what is in store for us. Here is hoping we have luck.

June 5, 1944

I feel like hell after General Quarters. Since last night 1745. After that first air raid everything was quiet until about one thirty A.M. when torpedo planes came in to attack us. One of the torpedo bombers was shot down. No hits were scored by the enemy after dropping approximately five torpedoes. Anti-aircraft fire went up quite a few times on the beach during the night. Probably Jap planes attacking army installations.

June 6, 1944

After patrolling in the area of Biak last night we set underway for Hollandia. Expect to get there 1900. Received news of the invasion of

Western France today. Invasion at 0500 G.C.T. three o'clock local time. Underway from Hollandia at 2315.

June 7, 1944

Headed for Biak again. Today I found out the real dope on that air raid of June fourth. Here it is. Forty-two planes, two engine heavies and single seater fighter bombers originally had started out to attack us that night, but only ten got through, as they were intercepted by our fighters. Their objective had been to completely demolish our force.

June 8, 1944

Reached the area of Biak tonight after a series of false air alerts this noon. At approximately 2340 we picked up five enemy ships.

Evidently these Jap ships didn't want to die for Tojo for they started running at a clip for thirty-two knots. Our force divided into two groups and we gave chase. A torpedo was seen streaking past our stern. We soon were left behind, but six "tin cans" gave chase. They were doing thirty-five knots. At this time we have no report yet. Reports indicated that they did not get within very good range. They damaged one destroyer.

June 10, 1944

Back to Hollandia after another all night of Condition IE. Picked up three to five ships last night and a battle was imminent, but we lost contact.

June 11, 1944

1630 underway from Hollandia for the Admiralties, Manus See-Adler Harbor.

June 12, 1944

Pulled into See-Adler Harbor in the Admiralties approximately 1540. Hope to get our much-needed rest now.

June 13, 1944

Today the Command of Task Force 74 left our area after having worked with us for the last six months. He is on the Australia. Don't know what is in store for us, but I think we will be moving out of this area also, within a very short time. Movie for tonight is "Kid Glove Killer" with Van Heflin and Marsha Hunt.

June 19, 1944

Went ashore and enjoyed a cold quart of beer and some "buck bathing," since we pulled into See-Adler Harbor. We are still hanging around. Suppose to get underway tomorrow.

CHAPTER 18

June 23, 1944

Still in the Admiralties. Got dope (scuttlebutt) that we have another invasion scheduled for the thirteenth or around then on the northern tip of New Guinea. Time will tell.

June 24, 1944

Just got off of the afternoon watch about an hour ago. Had one helluva lousy chow tonight. If the kid aside of me had not given me his fruit cocktail, I would probably have starved.

Just got finished taking a shower and then went to "sick bay" to get some salve for the "ringworm" I have got. Got a hell of a bad case on my "fanny" and all the scratching I do just makes it worse.

Well, tonight being Saturday night makes me long for those good old civilian days.

God knows when I will see them again. But here is hoping it's soon. I would certainly love to spend tonight dancing with Betty or Connie, a few drinks to round out the evening. Have to admit I am certainly feeling low right now. Well, I guess I will have to be content with seeing the movie aboard the ship tonight. The name is "Pied Piper" with Ann Baxter, what a doll. Also have the mid-watch 0000 to 0730 to look forward to.

We had Captain's inspection this morning in dungarees.

June 29, 1944

Got underway this morning 1130. Underway for another invasion. The Phoenix, Australia and Boise Cruisers.

June 30, 1944

Got a little dope from the executive officers speech today. "Dog Day" is the second of July. An island about sixty miles from Biak. Plans are similar to the previous invasions. So long for now. Suppose to fire 600 rounds of six inch and 500 rounds of five inch.

July 2, 1944

Number four Island. Invasion came off as scheduled this morning, approximately 0600 A.M. Everything worked smoothly as in previous operations. Troops received very little opposition. After our fairly heavy bombardment. About two hours after the first troops landed on the beach, it was announced they had captured the airstrip and advanced a few hundred yards beyond. Did not fire after the initial bombardment. Left the island about 1230. Right now we are on the way to Hollandia.

July 4, 1944

Underway from Hollandia for the Admiralties. 1000 PM.

July 5, 1944

Pulled into See-Adler Harbor approximately 1500 PM.

July 8, 1944

Saturday evening as I sit here in the compartment entering these few lines in my diary. The compartment is empty except for a few fellows sleeping in their sacks. Most of the fellows are at the movies, "Ball of Fire" with Barbara Stanwyk and Gary Cooper is playing. I saw the show a couple years ago. As usual I have the Saturday evening blues. Certainly would like to be back home right now. Well, think I will close now and write a couple letters. Got the mid-watch tonight Shropshire is back with us.

July 16, 1944

Still hanging around the Admiralties. Went out for AA practice once this week, but that's all. Played softball and basketball against the Army this week and won.

July 23, 1944

Still anchored in See-Adler Harbor in the Admiralties. I went ashore three times within the last week. Had six bottles of brew one day and four another day. Got a pretty good tan. Had quite a few good shows aboard within the last week. That's all for now.

July 26, 1944

Underway 0700. Another invasion coming up. Reports are that it will be pretty easy. Plans are that we don't do any firing.

July 30, 1944

Troops went ashore at approximately 0700 today at Sanspor Northwestern tip of New Guinea above Manokwari and about eighty miles from Sarong. The place was evacuated and we left at 1000 as our assistance was not needed. Troops that landed were Seabees. Their objective to build an airstrip, that's all.

July 31, 1944

Pulled into the harbor at Biak about 1200 today. Went ashore this afternoon. Had a pretty good time on the beach.

August 2, 1944

Went ashore this afternoon to explore the island and we came in contact with some natives on the island and had quite a time with them. We stole a couple of their canoes and also went through their huts.

August 3, 1944

Underway from Biak at 1830. Underway for Sydney, Australia. What a happy crew. WOW!!!! Happy Dreams.

August 6, 1944

Stopped off at Milne Bay yesterday after a rough day of it previously. Very rough the day before.

Underway at 1600 and ran into a bit of rough weather again. Reminds me of the good old Atlantic. Took about one hundred passengers aboard in Milne Bay. That's all. Bon Voyage.

August 7, 1944

Still bucking a heavy and rough sea. Lot of the boys are seasick. That's all.

CHAPTER 19

August 10, 1944

Pulled into Wooloomooloo landing Sydney at 0800.

Made my first liberty today. Having ten AM to nine PM o'clock liberty. Went over with Kanuch and Wilson and we started off at the Mayfair. Had a couple of beers there and then headed for the Adams Hotel. Had chow there and also had quite a few drinks. Kanuch got sick there. Headed for the Mayfair Lounge and could not get any drinks there, because the crowd was too loud. Mostly Boise men in here. Made it for downtown then. I was pretty "Jacked" by now. Stopped in at a milk bar for a few milk shakes and here I met one hell of a nice redhead. WOW!! She was working till 2200, so she asked me to come around tomorrow.

Decided to call up Patricia, a little gal I knew from the last time in Sydney. Dated her for 2000. Met her at the ferry landing. It was a dreadful night, so we went to a show. I just about slept thru it. Took her home to Mosman and found out she was pretty tough to crack so I hauled away and came back to the ship at 0130.

August 11, 1944

Got a shack on Springfield Ave. #9. Started out alone today. Met Kanuch and Wilson at Kings Cross. Had a couple drinks and just passed time away doing nothing. Left them at four o'clock. After drawing my liquor ration at the Naval station, went to the Trocadio large Ballroom on George St., met Gillian, Perkins, and Wartz and a lot of the crowd. Headed for the shack at 2300 after a disgusting evening. Dated redhead for Saturday evening.

August 12, 1944

Ashore with Kelm and Graphman today. Decided to go riding. Went to the Red Cross for information. Met a nice little "chick" in there and got her address. Finally got our destination at the Whitney riding school.

After a ten-minute cab ride I had one hell of a fast horse, as did Graphman, but Kelm got stuck with an old nag. Finished riding at two o'clock and we decided to go ice skating at the Glaciarium, a beautiful indoor rink. Had quite a time on the ice and was getting a might stiff by now. We went back to the shack and Kelm and I were dated for six-thirty.

Met the chicks on time and went for dinner at the Victorian. Headed for the "Roses" one of Sydney's fashionable night clubs. Slipped the waiter a pound, three dollars and twenty cents, and we got in. They soaked the hell out of us, but a good time was what we were after. Two pounds a pint of whiskey. Spend a hell of a happy four hours at "Roses" and we were all tight as hell. At one o'clock they closed up and we headed for home. No transportation this time of night, so we footed the girls to their apartments. Because of the strict rules about bringing any girls up to the flats, we tried to find a shack, but to no avail. We were still tight as hell when Kelm wheeled it over to the apartment. It seems red really went for me and I really did go for her. She talked of getting married, but we finally agreed upon waiting. Unable to leave each other we shacked up in a doorway. I got back to the flat at quarter to six and fell asleep, woke up at eight-thirty and had to be back at the ship by nine. So I got a cab and reached Wooloomoolo at five of nine. Still feeling like hell, as I write this and am a bit woozy, also got duty today, thank goodness. So long.

August 13, 1944

Duty today.

August 14, 1944

Ashore at 1100. Did not do very much during the day. Met Beryle at 2330 and we walked all the way to Kings Cross. Got in about 0200.

August 15, 1944

Ashore at 1100. Dinner with Beryl. Shopping in the afternoon. Met Beryl again at 2330. Had a midnight snack. Chicken Charmagne at a Chinese restaurant. Never ate such crude food in my life.

August 16, 1944

Ashore at 1100. Met Beryl at 1200, as we had a dinner date. Did not see Beryle after work tonight, as she has a pretty bad cold. So I called up Patricia and we took in a show. Got in about 0130. Got my liquor ration, one pint of Rum.

August 17 thru 23, 1944

Duty today. Washed my "blues" today. Saw Beryl Nolan every night and had quite a few dinner dates with her. We have become inseparable friends by now. Seems like we really are meant for each other. Had a blind date past Monday night….Really blind too!

Story goes I was supposed to have the duty, but Perkins got me off, as we had a couple of blind dates lined up. We went to the second best nightclub in Sydney at Romanos. Had a hell of a lousy time. Dates were not worth two cents.

Tuesday night the lady at Springfield Apartments gave a party for ten of us and we had a pretty good time.

August 24, 1944

My last liberty in Sydney. Met Beryl for a dinner date. Took in a show at seven and went to a hotel to spend the night in the lounge. Sat there and spent our last night together killing a pint of gin and a pint of rum.

We were slightly tight when we left at 0130. It was hard saying so long to Beryl. We were very much in love and I'll swear if it were not for the six months waiting period, we would be married by now. Boy, what a sweet gal. However, we have got plans for after the war. Who knows???

August 25, 1944

Duty today. Liberty expires on board at 2400 tonight. Meaning that we will be shoving off tomorrow, Saturday. I'm feeling pretty blue today knowing that I won't be seeing Beryl for a long time. That's about all.

August 26, 1944

Underway today at 0800. Pulling out of the harbor we were rammed by a tug and everyone was hoping for a delay, but it was only for a few hours.

CHAPTER 20

August 27, 1944

Pretty rough the first day out. Been getting all the sleep I can while the sleeping is good.

August 30, 1944

Milne Bay 0730 underway for See-Adler, Admiralty Islands at 1500. Weather getting hotter than hell.

September 2 to 9, 1944

Enter See-Adler Harbor. Still in See-Adler. New Jersey, Battleship was in a few days ago. Also twelve carriers are in at this time.

September 10, 1944

Underway at 0645. This looks like one of the biggest blows of the War, which we are headed for.

September 11, 1944

Pulled into Hollandia 0600. Underway at 2300.

September 12, 1944 D-Day 3

Still going smoothly. Destination is to be in the vicinity of Halmaherra. This will be a coordinated operation with third and fifth fleets. Other places hit will be Davo in the Philippines and Palau and Jap in the Carolines. Undoubtedly, this will be the biggest blow of the war in the Pacific.

September 13, 1944

Picked up our landing force last night sometime. Our Carrier force is also with us now. Today we moved along at Convoy speed about three to eight knots. D-day is Saturday Morning 0700 approximately.

September 14, 1944

Everything still going smoothly. Letting up NPM (fox) today.

September 15, 1944

Fireworks started at 0630 this Friday morning. We bombarded the northwestern tip of Halmaherra for approximately an hour. Barracks and airfield. Covered the target as well and started some fires. Then moved eight miles north of Halmaherra to Morotai Island to cover the landings. Very little opposition. General MacArthur is aboard the Cruiser Nashville.

Landing of Palau made by the third FIT was meeting pretty stiff opposition. Our landing on Morotai is about 300 miles south of the Philippines.

September 16, 1944

Our group CTF 75 was released today as no longer necessary in this section and at 1800 we headed for Biak Island.

September 17, 1944

Still underway. General Quarters at 2300. Couple bogus. We were just off of Numefoor Island and they were having an air raid there.

September 18, 1944

Pulled into Woendi an island not far from Biak Island at 0800; had morning watch. Going into four section.

September 24, 1944

Still at Biak Island. Went on beach few times in last week. No mail since leaving Manus.

September 27, 1944

0630 underway this morning from Biak Island with task force 74 and 75. I think? We are headed for See-Adler in the Admiralties.

September 29, 1944

Arrived at Admiralties.

September 30, 1944

Woke up this morning to find quite a bit of the third fleet in here.

October 5, 1944

Major ships in at present are: BATTLESHIPS: Idaho, Tennessee, Indiana, Pennsylvania, Mississippi, California, Maryland, West Virginia. CRUISERS: Nashville, Boise, Phoenix, Shropshire, Australia, Minneapolis, Honolulu, Portland, Indianapolis, Columbia, Denver, Louisville, Boston, Wichita, Camerra and Cleveland.

AIRCRAFT CARRIERS: (large) Hornet and approximately twenty to thirty small carriers and enumerable destroyers, destroyer escorts and patrol craft.

October 8, 1944

Went ashore a few times within the past week. Won five dollars on Navy over Penn State, but lost five on Notre Dame over Tulane, had twenty points.

Still at See-Adler, but think we are getting underway tomorrow or the next day, for good. Invasion of Philippines is a sure bet.

Well, might as well get this damn thing over with. Can't win the war sitting here in See-Adler. Got another injection yesterday. Don't know what for, but probably something to do with disease in Philippine area.

October 11, 1944

Underway for Hollandia at 1500 today.

October 12, 1944

Arrived at Hollandia 1200. Had movies aboard tonight. Think we shall pull out of here tomorrow. Refueled today.

I read the operations plan for the invasion coming up. Third fleet units will be operating with our seventh fleet. Five Battleships, California, Maryland, Mississippi, West Virginia, Pennsylvania and about six heavy Cruisers and six light with approximately fifteen Aircraft Carriers. We are striking at the central Philippines. Name of the place is Leyte about 200 miles below Manila. Looks like one hell of an operation. Here is to luck.

October 13, 1944

Underway at 1600 from Hollandia. Got quite a force of transports with us. I learned that there are to be 54 large transports in the fleet. That is not counting the LST and LCI's and smaller craft. These fifty-four transports alone amount to about 250,000 men.

October 14, 1944

Everything going smoothly

October 15, 1944

Joined up with the other force of transports and battlewagons and cruisers this morning.

Got two more shots this morning. One for Cholera and the other for Tetanus.

October 18, 1944

Everything is still going smoothly. This morning we were about 450 miles from the Philippines doing about eight knots. D-day is Friday morning.

Have been listening to Tokyo broadcast past few days and they have been putting out reports that our invasion force has been annihilated and other fantastic reports. That's all for now. Have the mid-watch tonight.

October 19, 1944

Everything still going smoothly.

October 20, 1944

Pulled into Leyte Bay early this morning after rendezvousing with the other task forces. We barely moved during the night, as we were but twenty-five miles from the beaches. At daybreak hell, havoc broke loose. Went to General Quarters at approximately two in the morning. At daybreak the Japs started coming over. We received about seven or eight bombs right around us. The destroyer Ross took a bomb hit and also a transport. The battleship started this bombardment at about seven and bombarded for a half-hour. Then we went in. After that the first wave went in. We had established a firm beachhead by noon.

Had a few air raids in the afternoon. A torpedo bomber scored a hit on the Honolulu C48.

October 21, 1944

At daybreak this morning we had another attack, air, we shot down a couple planes and one of the planes crashed into the HMAS Australia. Had about four more attacks during the day. At five in the afternoon we got reports that the Japs were underway with about fifteen transports and TF74 and 75.

October 22, 1944

Another air attack at dawn. We had quite a bit of firing, but scored no hits.

October 24, 1944

Had the mid-watch last night. Japs really played hell today. Started off with General Quarters at 0730. Went to General Quarters about ten times during the day. Waves of twenty and 11 planes came over for an attack, but were intercepted by our fighters who shot approximately twenty to twenty-five down.

We got these order for each day:

U.S.S. BOISE

24 October 1944

ORDERS FOR THE DAY—WEDNESDAY, 25 OCTOBER, 1944

DUTY HEAD OF DEPARTMENT—Comdr. Cassidy

DUTY SECTION: 1st
DUTY DIVISION: 4th

UNIFORM OF THE DAY—OFFICERS RS & CPO'S: Khaki without ties.
                                     ENLISTED MEN: Dungarees with
                                                            shirts, blue hats

0000	-	Execute ship's routine with the following substitutions and additions.
0500	-	All hands.
0530	-	Precautionary General Quarters.
1630	-	Sunrise. Light ship. Secure from General Quarters.
0700	-	Breakfast
0830	-	Muster on stations

1700	-	All divisions check condition settings and make report to the Damage Control Office.
	-	Sunset. Darken ship.
NOTES:		(1) Water consumed for the previous 24 hours was 18.9 gallons per man.

From: 14th INFANT. DIV.

To: NAVAL GUN CONTROLLER ON FREMONT.

Learned from G1 this morning that certain ships have done so well that they should be told of their success by a responsible party. Would you care to take the few remarks that we have and pass them on to the ships. The ships are BOISE, PHOENIX BEALE. PHOENIX eliminated obstacles in the way of our advance in the area, although they naturally failed to knock out pillboxes and dug in positions. Anti-personnel effect was excellent. BOISE yesterday afternoon destroyed large numbers of enemy personnel, although failing to know out pill boxes which would have required direct hits, but this is no criticism of them. She was observed blowing 2 Japs to bits as they emerged from a dug in position. BEALE fired well generally, but have no details of the result.

- - - - - - - - -

From: SHORE FIRE CONTROL PART #3.

To: 24TH INFANT. DIV.

I was told another concentration of enemy fire was placed on our mortar and infantry position during the night. It is true, it is not, that BOISE has been doing most of your firing and they should be commended. Yesterday BOISE covered town areas with fire. Very effective on exposed personnel. The only things not knocked out were the pillboxes, which would have required direct hits.

- - - - - - - - -

T. M. WOLVERTON,
Comdr., U.S. Navy,
Executive Officer.

October 25, 1944

Last night it happened; we received reports of Jap surface not very far from Leyte. At 1000 we left the Gulf of Leyte with six wagons, four light cruisers and five heavies and twenty-five destroyers. We picked up contact at approximately 2330 to 0100. The action started at 0345. The Cans and PT's went in first and fired flares and then let loose with the Tin Fish. After that we, cruiser and batterywagon opened up. We scored quite a few hits on a Wagon and another presumably a cruiser. Have not got any straight dope yet, but a Jap prisoner picked up by one of our ships said that we got two battleships and six smaller ships, presumably Cans or CL. One of our destroyers was shot up pretty badly. Couple of the cruisers were straddled, but otherwise we did all right. At dawn we saw a crippled battlewagon on the horizon and it went down. Oil covered the battle area for miles around. What a night. Hope to hell I never have to go through anything like it again.

Official results of the surface engagement on the night or early morning of October twenty-fifth was two Battleships, two Cruisers, one light and one heavy and six destroyers.

Tonight we got underway again with the same force we had the night previous. Quite a few Jap Task Forces are hanging around here.

Our bombers attacked a task force of four wagons and other ships. They badly damaged the largest wagon.

Reports are that a task force of four battleships and eight heavy cruisers and many destroyers are headed up toward us from Mindoro in the southern Philippines.

Hackey, commander of the third fleet is reported to be sending us six more battlewagons and three large new carriers.

Here is hoping, so we probably will be making good use of them.

Our task force shot down about seven planes today. Haven't had more than five hours sleep in the last three days. It is about 1900 right now and unless we make contact tonight I'll have all night in.

Here to lunch and may we not run into any trouble tonight and if we do, may we have all the protection and success we had last night.

More tomorrow. I would give a million to be back home right now.

October 26, 1944

Everything okay tonight. No surface, most of the remaining Jap forces were sunk by our Air Force and escaped through the strait.

Philippines Island invasion: Surragio Straits (surface engagement) probably one of the greatest in history. Wiped out a force of two battleships, two Cruisers and six Destroyers and damaged a Cruiser and more Destroyers.

October 27, 1944

Early this morning we joined a force of six Carriers. Nashville and Boise and ten destroyers. Phoenix and Shropshire took charge of another force of Carriers. This is no striking force, but a "scouting force."

October 28, 1944

This morning we received orders to return to Leyte Gulf minus the carriers. Presumably to join the other force of BB and Cruisers. Received a dispatch this morning that Leyte had been secured and the last resistance ceased. Scuttlebutt is that we are making an invasion of another island in the Philippines group in a few days. Nine destroyers left for the States today. The BB Tennessee also pulled out. She received a close miss the other night and received a large hole in the hull.

We are now operating in a new task group. Same as the original Task Force 75, but have added the Battleships and Pennsylvania and Mississippi and California.

Things have been very quiet the past few days.

November 1, 1944

Rather be going out on the first day of hunting season back home now, instead of being up here in the Philippines.

Hell havoc broke loose again yesterday. The Japs sent "suicide pilots" in one and two at a time yesterday on our Task Force. This force (special) is a suicide squadron, which deliberately dives into a ship for the Glory of dying for their country. They crashed five of our destroyers this way yesterday. The Abner Read was sunk in this manner shortly after noon yesterday. There also is another Jap Task Force hanging around. We shot down quite a few planes yesterday, although the Japs really took a toll of our ships.

November 17, 1944

Left for Manus, also got mail today.

November 20, 1944

Got into the Admiralties, Manus Island.

November 28, 1944

Underway approximately 1800 today. Presumably for Leyte in the Philippines. Have been ashore two times during our stay here in Manus.

December 1, 1944

Pulled into Leyte Gulf early this morning. During our absence from Leyte three destroyers were sunk, the St. Louis was hit by suicide planes a "special attack corp" and the Battleship Colorado received a near miss. Looks like we might have a nice time of it.

December 2, 1944

Tonight we had a narrow escape from a torpedo plane. The plane came in low after sundown and was never spotted by any of the ships. He dropped his "fish" just passing off our stern.

December 3, 1944

Today the Battleships West Virginia, Colorado, Maryland and New Mexico pulled out and also a couple heavy and light Cruisers. No air attacks today.

December 5, 1944

Tonight we were attacked by about six Jap dive-bombers. We, Boise, alone shot down two of them and the others did not carry out their attacks.

December 8, 1944

The past few nights we spent in the Harbor of Leyte. We sent four of our destroyers up to Ormoc Bay to bombard positions and one was sunk and one badly damaged; however, our destroyers accounted for a couple of our destroyers and some barges and bombarded shore installations. Night of December eighth we landed forces around Ormoc Bay area. Our Air Force also sank a convoy of thirteen Jap ships. Presumably trying to reinforce troops in the Ormoc section.

December 9, 1944

Underway around noon today Phoenix, Boise, four destroyers to relieve one patrol in the Gulf.

CHAPTER 21

December 12, 1944

Underway this afternoon about 1500 for the invasion of Mindaro Island in the Philippines. Northernmost tip of the island, incidentally is about fifty miles out of Manila.

December 13, 1944

Joined up with the convoy today. Mostly LCIS and LSTs. Four Cruisers—Nashville, Phoenix, Portland (ca), Boise. Another force consisting of four (CVE) Carriers, four Cruisers and four Battleships are going to cover our group by scouting for us. Air attacks started at ten o'clock this morning. About six planes attacked. No hit, no errors. About two this afternoon the Nashville was crash-dived by a Jap plane. We stayed at General Quarters for about seven hours. Quite a few planes were shot down by our "fighter cover" of P-38 and Navy Carrier planes.

We were missed by a couple bombs and the plane shot down by a P-38 landed just astern of us. We were under constant attack.

December 14, 1944

Today was unseemly quiet. No real attacks so far. Went to General Quarters about six times though. Tomorrow the landing comes off. Invasion of Mindoro. Here is to luck and great success.

December 15, 1944

Invasion of Mindoro took place today. The actual invasion was practically unopposed due to the surprise landing. About ten o'clock enemy planes started coming over. During the day approximately twenty to thirty planes were shot down by attack and fighters. The "Kamihari Boys" crashed dived and destroyed two LST's. Otherwise our ships suffered no damage the first day.

December 16, 1944

Underway for Leyte after picking up convoy about 100 miles out of Mindaro.

December 17, 1944

Arrived Leyte Gulf about 0930. About 1830 the Nashville got underway, presumably for the States.

December 18, 1944

Still anchored in the harbor at Leyte. Having air raids quite frequently. In fact, about six to twelve a day.

December 25, 1944

Christmas, had good meal today. Slept most of the day though, I had no sleep for about thirty hours.

December 26, 1944

Got underway at six tonight. Phoenix, Boise, Minneapolis and Louisville (heavies) and about ten destroyers. Underway for Mindoro as reports are that a Jap Battlewagon and several Cruisers and Destroyers are headed that way. So we might see a little action.

December 27, 1944

Arrived at Mindoro, too late, however, as the Japs bombarded this place for about three hours last night.

December 28, 1944

We patrolled the southern tip of Mindoro all during the night. Made several surface contacts, but they turned out to be friendly PT Boats. Tonight at six we started a high speed run twenty-six knots for Leyte.

December 29, 1944

Arrived at Leyte Gulf about three this afternoon.

December 30, 1944

Put on report for being out of uniform.

CHAPTER 22

January 3, 1945

For the past week we have been making preparations for General MacArthur, Admiral Kinchaid and a couple of high Army Officials to come aboard for the coming operation.

January 4, 1945

General MacArthur and three other One Star Generals came aboard this afternoon. Underway at 1534.

January 6, 1945

Contacted a submarine this afternoon. Two torpedos were fired at us, but passed quite a ways astern of us.

January 7, 1945

Planes attacked today. Two were shot down by our force. Tonight we had a surface contact, which turned out to be a Jap destroyer. We sent our destroyers out after it and they sank it in very little time.

January 8, 1945

The Japs attacked our convoy of transports and task force again this morning. We got two more planes. I was manning a tactical maneuvering circuit on the bridge and saw the twin motor Bomber (Betty) go down a couple hundred yards off our port beam. Evidently, he was trying to crash-dive one of our "Cans."

January 9, 1945

Well, today the landing took place at some bay about a hundred miles above Manila on Luzon in the Philippines. Luigayen Gulf, the site of the landing. The landings met little resistance. General Quarters will finish later. Just secured from General Quarters. Jap Kamakasa Corp crash dive experts sure played hell with our Navy. In the last few days the following Cruisers were hit, Columbia two times, Australia two times, Shropshire two times, Louisville (Ca), Mississippi and California Battlewagons.

January 10, 1945

Last night the Japs attacked our shipping in the Harbor. They sank and LST and LCI and a large transport APA and damaged a couple destroyers and an LST. We had quite a time.

January 13, 1945

For the past three to four days we have been anchored in the harbor and have been under constant air attack by the Japs. Almost every day they damaged a couple of our ships. This afternoon MacArthur and his staff finally left the ship. We will probably get underway.

The following letter was left for us:

GENERAL HEADQUARTERS
SOUTHWEST PACIFIC AREA
Office of the Commander-in-Chief

8 January 1945

Dear Captain Downes:

Before disembarking from the BOISE I wish to offer my high commendation of the outstanding manner in which you and your officers and crew have participated in the restoration of our flag in the Philippines.

Your highly professional seamanship and the magnificent discipline and fighting spirit of your crew in hazardous circumstances have fully upheld the high traditions of the United States Navy.

For myself and my staff I thank you for the many courtesies we have enjoyed during the time the BOISE has served as my headquarters afloat.

With my sincere appreciation of a job well done.

Faithfully yours,

DOUGLAS MacARTHUR.

The following are our orders for the day:

U.S.S. BOISE

13 January 1945

ORDERS FOR THE DAY—SUNDAY, 14 JANUARY 1945

DUTY HEAD OF DEPARTMENT—Commander Whitaker—Until 1200.
Commander Cassidy—Until 1200.

DUTY SECTION: 1ST
DUTY DIVISION: 1ST

UNITFORM OF THE DAY—OFFICERS & CPO'S: Khaki without ties, long trousers.

ENLISTED MEN: Dungarees with shirts (sleeves Rolled down), blue hats.

0000	-	Execute ship's routine with the following substitutions and additions.
0530	-	All hands.
0630	-	Precautionary General Quarters.
0730	-	Sunrise. Light ship.
0735	-	Breakfast.
0830	-	Muster on stations.
1700	-	All divisions check condition settings and make report to the Damage Control Office.
	-	Sunset. Darken ship.

NOTES: (1) Water consumed for the previous 24 hours was 17.5 gallons per man.

(2) Two hands each from the deck divisions and three hands from the Engineering force report to HOLLOWELL, SK3c, in the Main Issue Room at 0800.

(3) General MacArthur left an autographed photograph for
the BOISE. Duplicate copies of the photo will be made on
the same order as were the Christmas cards for distribu-
tion to the crew.

> E. T. EVES,
> Comdr., U.S. Navy,
> Executive Officer.

January 14, 1945

We refueled at midnight and got underway at about 0100. Today at
about 1100 we joined three CVE small Carriers the Phoenix,
Montapelier, Denver and about eight Cans. Patrolling about eighty to a
hundred miles out of Manila.

January 16, 1945

Still operating with the Carriers.

January 18, 1945

Headed for Mindoro tonight.

January 19, 1945

Pulled into Mindoro today. Refueled and got mail tonight. Pulled out
about 2400 to rejoin the Carriers.

January 22, 1945

Still on patrol in the China Sea off the coast of Luzon with the
Carriers (4-CVE) and our Cruisers.

January 28, 1945

Covered the landing near San Antonio on Luzon.

February 1, 1945

Back to Mindoro. Looks like there is a possibility of our going back.
Here is hoping.

USS BOISE CREW

1945

SUBIC BAY, PHILIPPINE ISLAND

February 8, 1945

Underway from Mindoro for Subic Bay. 1830.

February 9, 1945

Enter Subic Bay about 1000.

February 13, 1945

Underway at 0545 for the bombardment of Corregidor and Bataan. The Cruisers Montipelier, Denver, Phoenix, Cleveland and of course the old reliable Boise. Started bombarding about 1030. Planes coordinated with our Naval bombardment. Had no return fire from any shore batteries. No opposition from the mighty fortress of Corregidor and Bataan. After pouring about three hundred rounds of six inch and two hundred and fifty round of five inch into the fortresses, we left for Subic Bay at 0130. Incidentally, Subic Bay in only about a thirty-five mile distance.

We had movies at Subic Bay.

February 14, 1945

Underway for Corregidor and Bataan again at 0545. Started bombardment at approximately 0915. Only today there was quite a bit of excitement. We put out about 600 six inch and probably more five inch steel.

A few ships were hit by shore batteries today. In fact, they were throwing steel back at us all day. Two destroyers hit mines and were pretty badly damaged. One minesweeper was sunk, another "Can" was hit by shore batteries. We also scored a few hits on a small Coastal Steamer. Quite a day.

We pulled out—Cleveland and Boise for Subic Bay at 1830.

Might have movies tonight, if we get back in time. Incidentally, the last four nights we have been having movies topside, while about fifteen miles inland the doughboys and Japs are ferociously slugging it out. Artillery, gun flashes are easily visible. Tomorrow we are landing troops on Bataan.

February 15, 1945

Troops went ashore on Bataan today. Very little opposition. We did not put out too many rounds today. Had very little trouble from shore batteries today. P-38, P-47, A-20 and B-24 liberators gave Corregidor another unmerciful pounding today.

February 16, 1945

This morning troops hit Corregidor. About 0810 a fleet of C-47s dropped about 1200 Airborne troops and later on, Amphibs landed. We did not fire today.

February 17, 1945

After patrolling between Subic Bay and Corregidor we again took station for Call-fire. Did not fire there.

1800 we started out for Subic. Arrived Subic Bay 0745. Taking on fuel tonight. Incidentally, this has been the fourth day of all-day General Quarters for us.

Hope we have some mail!!!

February 19, 1945

Enter Subic Bay.

February 25, 1945

Underway for Lingayen Gulf. (2000).

February 26, 1945

Enter Lingayen Bay (900).

March 1, 1945

Back to Subic Bay, Philippines.

March 7, 1945

Left Subic Bay and left Mindoro respectively. By the eighth of March we start the pre-invasion bombardment of Zamoanga on the south-western tip of Mindanao in the Philippines. Landing is to be the tenth of March.

March 10, 1945

After two days of pre-invasion bombardment troops went ashore this morning at 0915. We knocked out a hell of a lot of gun positions in our bombardment. Looks like the seventh fleet did it again. Phoenix and Boise.

March 11, 1945

More bombarding today.

March 12, 1945

Everything going fine. Did not bombard today. Pulled out tonight at 800 for Mindoro.

March 13, 1945

Made a few trips between Mindoro and Subic Bay between this period of time. Covered the Cebu operation.

April 3, 1945

U.S.S. BOISE

3 April 1945

ORDERS FOR THE DAY—WEDNESDAY, 4 APRIL 1945

DUTY HEAD OF DEPARTMENT—Commander Beardslee—Until 1200.
Commander Whitaker—Until 1200.

DUTY SECTION: 3rd
DUTY DIVISION: 3rd

UNIFORM OF THE DAY—OFFICERS & CPO'S: Khaki without ties, long trousers or shorts.

ENLISTED MEN: Dungarees with or without shirts, blue hats.

0000	-	Execute ship's routine with the following substitutions and additions.
0445	-	Make all preparations for getting underway.
0515	-	All hands.
	-	Station the special sea detail.
0545	-	Underway for Manila.
0652	-	Sunrise. Light ship.
0700	-	Breakfast.
0800	-	Turn to.
0830	-	Muster on stations.
	-	Anchor Manila.
0900	-	Morning sight seeing party to ready to leave the ship.
1300	-	1st party return—Dinner.
1330	-	2nd party to be ready to leave ship.
1730	-	2nd party return.
1800	-	All divisions check condition settings and make report to the Damage Control Office.

NOTES: (1) Water consumed for the previous 24 hours was 21.4 gallons per man.

(2) The ship is going to Manila in order that all hands may
have an opportunity to make a tour of the city and
actually see the damage before reconstruction begins.
This tour is not a recreation party and all hands are in a
duty status. Conduct yourselves so that no criticism
attaches to the BOISE and so that future tours of this
kind will not be jeopardized. You will remain with the
group at all times, do not straggle or leave the group for
any purpose. Men on the restricted list may make the
tour and only those who previously made it or are in
the brig now are ineligible.

E. T. EVES,
Commander, U.S. Navy
Executive Officer.

April 4, 1945

Underway for Manila this morning. Got ashore for a few hours in
Manila. Strictly a sight seeing party with an officer in charge. Philippine
girls really "stacked up" in Manila.

Stayed in Manila Harbor for two days. Harbor is really a mass of
sunken Japanese ships. Must be hundreds.

April 6, 1945

Underway 1700 for Leyte. Boise and about four destroyers first leg of
trip to Manus. Going in dry dock at Manus.

April 8, 1945

Pulled into Leyte Harbor this Sunday morning approximately 0900.
Underway Leyte 1800 for Manus. First time in Leyte since the Lingayen
operation.

April 11, 1945

Anchored See-Adler Harbor 1700 today, Wednesday. Incidentally, this has been our first time here since Last November twenty-sixth. We are going into dry dock tomorrow, I think. Manus is practically deserted. Very few ships in here.

The following was issued today:

COMMANDER SERVICE FORCE
SEVENTH FLEET

11 April 1945.

SERVICE FORCE, SEVENTH FLEET, COURT-MARTIAL ORDER
NO. 28-45.

1. Joseph H. Swartz, storekeeper third class U.S. Naval Reserve, was tried by a general court martial at the Commander Service Force, Seventh Fleet, on the following charges and specifications:

   CHARGE I   CONSPIRACY (1 specification)

   The specification pertained to conspiring to steal ten cases of beer, property of the United States.

   CHARGE II   WRONGFULLY AND KNOWINGLY SELL PROPERTY OF THE UNITED STATES INTEDED FOR THE NAVAL SERVICE THEREFORE (1 specification)

   The specification pertained to selling ten cases of beer, property of the United States, to certain Army personnel.

   CHARGE III   WRONGFULLY AND KNOWINGLY DISPOSE OF PROPERTY OF THE UNITED STATES INTENDED FOR THE NAVAL SERVICE THEREOF (1 specification)

   The specification pertained to conspiring to disposing of ten cases of beer, property of the United States, to certain Army personnel.

CHARGE IV   KNOWINGLY AND WILLFULLY APPLY TO HIS OWN USE PROPERTY OF THE UNITED STATES INTENDED FOR THE NAVAL SERVICE THEREOF (1 specification)

The specification pertained to conspiring to supplying to his own use two cases of beer, property of the United States.

2. The accused was acquitted of Charges I and II, and the specifications thereunder, and was found guilty of Charges III and IV and the specifications, thereunder.

3. The court sentenced the accused to be reduced to the rating of apprentice seaman, to be confined for a period of six months, and to suffer all the other accessories of said sentence as prescribed by Section 622, Naval Courts and Boards.

4. On April 9, 1945, the convening authority approved the proceedings, the findings on Charges I, II and III, and the specifications thereunder, and the sentence in this case, and disapproved the finding on Charge IV and the specification thereunder.

5. The Naval Annex of the U.S. Army round Mountain Detention and Rehabilitation Center, Queensland, Australia, was designated as the place for the execution of so much of the sentence as relates to confinement.

> Robert O. Glover,
> Rear Admiral, U.S. Navy
> Commander Service Force,
> Seventh Fleet.

E. N. BUDDRESS,
Flag Secretary.

April 13, 1945

Received shattering news this morning. The President of the United States, Franklin D. Roosevelt, died of a cerebral hemorrhage at his Hot Springs, Georgia vacation home.

April 15, 1945

Out of dry-dock this morning. Under 1800 after loading store all day.

April 18, 1945

Enter Leyte. Underway Leyte 1800 for Subic Bay. MacArthur's flagstaff came aboard at Leyte. Also think Admiral Kinkaid, Commander of the seventh fleet is coming aboard.

April 21, 1945

Enter Subic Bay this morning.

April 24, 1945

Underway today. Operation of Tarakan ahead of us. Tarakan is a small island just off the mainland of Borneo in the Dutch East Indies. Small operation.

April 26, 1945

Our orders for the day:

U.S.S. BOISE

25 April 1945

ORDERS FOR THE DAY—THURSDAY, 26 APRIL 1945.

DUTY HEAD OF DEPARTMENT—Commander Whitaker—Until 1200.
Commander Cassidy—After 1200.

DUTY SECTION: 1ST
DUTY DIVISION: 1ST

UNIFORM OF THE DAY—OFFICERS & COP'S: Khaki without ties, long trousers.
ENLISTED MEN: Dungarees with shirts, blue hats. Sleeves rolled down.

0000 - Execute ship's routine with the following substitutions and additions.
0530 - All hands.
0555 - Precautionary General Quarters.
0655 - Sunrise. Light ship. Secure from General Quarters.
0730 - Breakfast.
0800 - Turn to.
0830 - Muster on stations.
      - The 1st division report forward of turret I for instruction on "All Purpose Nozzles and CO2 Extinguishers."
      - The 2nd division report to the port side of turret I for instruction in "All Purpose Nozzles and CO2 Extinguishers."
      - The 3rd division report to the starboard side of turret I for instructions in "Nomenclature and Numbering of Decks and Compartments."
      - The 4th division report to the starboard side of turret II for instruction in "Nomenclature of Numbering of Decks and Compartments."

	-	Shore Bombardment Drill for Main Battery.—Lieut. PICKENS.
	-	Recognition instruction for 7th division lookouts and 5th division I the Mess Hall.
0930	-	Shore Bombardment Drill for Secondary Batter.—Lieut. FARRI.
	-	The 5th and 6th divisions report to the port side of turret IV for instruction in the "Duplex Liquid Foam Proportioner."
	-	The 7th division report to the port side of turret I for instruction in the "Rescue Breathing Apparatus."
1015	-	Recognition for 6th division lookouts in Mess Hall.
1100	-	Recognition instruction for officers in the Wardroom.
1300	-	All men in the 1st and 2nd divisions who had the 08-12 watch report forward of turret I for instruction in "All Purpose Nozzles and C02 Extinguishers."
	-	All men in the 5th and 6th divisions who had the 08-12 watch report to port side of turret IV for instruction in the "Duplex Liquid Foam Pressure Proportioner."
	-	All men in the 3rd and 4th divisions who had the 08-12 watch report to port side of turret I for instruction in "Nomenclature and Numbering of Decks and Compartments."
	-	All men in the 7th division who had the 08-12 watch report to the starboard side of turret II for instruction in the "Rescue Breathing Apparatus."
1700	-	All divisions check condition settings and make report to the Damage Control Office.

NOTES:

(1) Water consumed for the previous 24 hours was 16.4 gallons per man.

(2) Mess cooks report to VOLNER, BrkLc, in the hangar at 0900.

(3) 6 hands report to INGOLD, SC2c, in hangar at 0830.

(4) Any person desiring to join the Ship's Orchestra please turn in your name at the Library.

(5) For the next week we will be operating within range of enemy aircraft and off the coast of Borneo. All hands are cautioned to wear full uniform with sleeves rolled down and to be alert on watch.

> E. T. EVES,
> Commander, U.S. Navy,
> Executive Officer.

April 28, 1945

For the past two days we have been "standing off Borneo" waiting to make a landing. Everything quiet.

April 30, 1945

Today Aussie troops, small number, went ashore on Sadua Island. Mostly engineers to clean up the beach area. Very little opposition.

May 1, 1945

Today Aussies troops went ashore on Tarakan Island off Borneo. This island is right in oil and before the War produced 9,000,000 barrels per year. Very little opposition.

May 2, 1945

Still hanging around Borneo. Fired about fifty rounds today.

May 3, 1945

Still hanging around Borneo.

May 4, 1945

Underway 1300 today, evidently for Subic and to pick up MacArthur. I also learned that a few Jap planes raided the dry docks at Manus in the Admiralties. They damaged both dry docks. Same docks we were in a few weeks previously.

May 15, 1945

U.S.S. Nashville pulled into Subic Bay this morning.

CHAPTER 23

May 17, 1945

Tonight we received the most wonderful news anyone, I suppose, has ever heard. The Captain announced that we were going back to the States on JULY twenty-sixth. The twenty-sixth of next month.

At the time of the announcement over the "PA" system I was sitting back on the fantail reading (about 1800). The guys were jumping up and down, smiles a mile wide covered every face. I just got a few words of the announcement and I gathered that the war had ended. Could not sleep last night for about three hours. Just lay in my sack and thought how good it will be to get home again. Um!!!!!!!!!!!

Here is hoping the time passes swiftly and here is to the day we get underway for the States!!!!

May 22, 1945

Nashville, Phoenix and the Boise underway 0615 this morning for Manila and liberty. I do not rate today.

May 23, 1945

Liberty 1200 to 1800. Sold my watch for sixty bucks.

May 25, 1945

Liberty Manila. Sold carton cigarettes for six dollars.

May 26, 1945

Underway Subic 0730.

May 27, 1945

Enter Subic 1215 noon.

May 28, 1945

Still in Subic.

May 29, 1945

Getting closer to July twenty-sixth.

May 31, 1945

Underway for Manila tomorrow.

June 1, 1945

Reached Manila 1200 today.

June 3, 1945

General Douglas MacArthur came aboard tonight 1730. Underway.

June 4, 1945

Arrive at Mindoro and anchor 0809.

June 5, 1945

Anchor Cagayan 0800 northern tip of Mindanoa, 1830.

June 6, 1945

Anchor Cebu 0800. Underway 1400. Beautiful country.

June 7, 1945

Anchor Slolo, Panay 0730 underway 1800.

June 8, 1945

Anchor Palawan 0830. Underway 1800. Picked up Kinney Four Star General Commander of airforces far east.

June 10, 1945

Land troops of Burniu, west coast of Borneo. Our last operation before we hit the states. Not much opposition this far. Put out approximately 1003 rounds six-inch and 800 rounds five-inch.

June 11, 1945

Underway from Borneo. 1300.

June 12, 1945

Anchor Jolooff of Mindanao 1300. Many small native outriggers, hundreds of them, came out to meet us. Underway 1600.

June 13, 1945

Anchor Davao, Mindanao, 1100. Underway 1600.

June 14, 1945

1800 anchor Zamboanga, Mindanao, Philippines. Underway 1200.

June 15, 1945

Anchor Manila 1000. General MacArthur detached from ship. Won't be long now.
Received a dispatch from the Commander in Chief.

15 June 1945

The Commanding Officer takes a great deal of pride in quoting the following dispatch received from the Commander in Chief, Southwest Pacific Area.

"PLEASE ACCEPT FOR YOURSELF AND EXPRESS TO YOUR COM-
MANDERS, OFFICERS AND MEN MY HEATIEST CONGRATUALA-
TIONS FOR THE FLAWLESS PERFORMANCE OF THE DIFFICULT
AND DANGEROUS MISSION ASSIGNED YOU TASK FORCE IN
CONNECTION WITH THE EXECUTION OF OBOE 6. THE "BOISE,"
THE "KILLEN," AND THE "GRANT" HAVE ADDED LUSTER TO
THEIR SPLENDID RECORDS OF BATTLE AND CAMPAIGN SER-
VICE IN THE SOUTHWEST PACIFIC."

SIGNET MACARTHUR

The Commanding Officer wishes to add "Well Done" to all officers and men of
the BOISE. General MacArthur's final words to me this morning as he left the
ship were, "May God be with you and your magnificent ship until we meet
again."

W. M. DOWNES

June 16, 1945

Underway 2100 from Manila for United States. Leyte indirectly.

June 18, 1945

Enter Leyte 0800. Large fleet gathered in the harbor here. Many large
battleships, cruisers and large aircraft carriers.

Underway from Leyte 1330 for Pearl Harbor at sixteen knots.
Weather getting a little rough. Richter and Lowe now on the Astoria
came aboard to visit for a few hours. Tonight I put my name in for a
transfer when we hit the States. Ticonderoga, aircraft carrier was in
Leyte.

June 26, 1945

Cross the International Date Line tomorrow (180 Meridan) morning.
Lose twenty-four hours, day reverts back to the twenty-sixth. Smooth
sailing thus far.

June 29, 1945

Enter Naval Base of Pearl Harbor Hawaiian Island. Hornet and Saratoga also enter same time.

Band and all playing for us on the dock. Quite a place.

June 30, 1945

Went ashore today liberty from nine to one. Went into the city of Honolulu, which is about 20 miles from the descrupae landing. Only had about an hour and a half in town, but city is very clean. People seem very civilized and you can buy anything you want for reasonable prices.

First thing I did was get some chow. Eggs, sunny side up, hot cakes and a quart of milk, banana split and a coke. Got a few souvenirs.

Underway this afternoon at 1415 for San Pedro, California. State side, here we come!!!!!!

July 7, 1945

San Pedro at LAST! Pulled in here approximately at six this morning. Took us until 1834 to unload the ammunition. No liberty granted tonight. Have the duty tomorrow. So until then. THE END!!!!!!

JULY 9, 1945 THE HOLLYWOOD PALLADIUM

ARMSTRONG—N.Y. CHALMERS HALLMAN—PA.

JOSEPH E. GASKE—CHICAGO

Chalmers Hallman taken on the Boise in the Atlantic Ocean in 1945

The war was over and we were transporting Army troops home from France.

'One-ship Fleet' Arrives in New York Harbor

Against a backdrop of Manhattan skyline, the light cruiser U.S.S. Boise slips into New York harbor to take her place among the growing armada of vessels gathering for the mighty Presidential review on Navy Day, Oct. 27. The fighting ship earned her proud sobriquet of "one-ship task force" in her first major battle-off Cape Esperance on Oct. 11 and 12, 1942-where she sank four destroyers and two cruisers. Aboard the vessel were 440 Army personnel, the first such to be returned to New York by warship.

Dictionary of American Naval Fighting Ships

Office of the Chief of Naval Operations
Naval History Division • Washington

USS *Boise* (CL-47)

A city in Idaho.

(CL-47: dp. 9700; 1. 60S'4"; b. 61'9", dr. 24', s. 33.5 k.; cpl. 868; a. 15 6", 8 5"; cl. *Brooklyn*) *Boise* (CL-477) was launched 3 December 1936 by Newport News Shipbuilding and Dry Dock Co., Newport News, Va.; sponsored by Miss Salome Clark, daughter of Governor Clark of Idaho, and commissioned 12 August 1938, Captain B. V. McCandlish in command.

In February 1939, following a shakedown cruise to Monrovia, Liberia; and Cape Town, Union of South Africa, *Boise* joined Division 9, Cruisers Battle Force, at San Pedro, Calif. Until November 1941 she operated alternately off the west coast and in Hawaiian waters. She then escorted a convoy to Manila, Philippine Islands, arriving 4 December 1941.

The outbreak of war in the Philippines, 8 December 1941, found *Boise* off Cebu. She joined TF 5 in the East Indies, but on 21 January 1942 struck an uncharted shoal in Sape Strait and had to retire to Colombo, Ceylon; Bombay, India; and Mare Island Navy Yard for repairs. Her repairs completed, she sailed 22 June 1942 to escort a convoy to Auckland, New Zealand. She then returned to Pearl Harbor and during 11 July-10 August 1942 conducted a raiding cruise in Japanese waters as a feint to draw attention away from the Guadalcanal landings. In August she escorted a convoy to the Fiji and New Hebrides Islands. During 1-18 September she helped cover the landing of Marine reinforcements on Guadalcanal. In the succeeding hard fighting she was hit by Japanese shells in the American victory of **Cape Esperance** after taking six planes under fire. She made her way to Philadelphia Navy Yard where she underwent repairs (19 November 1942–20 March 1943).

Boise departed 8 June 1943 for the Mediterranean, arriving at Algiers, Algeria, 21 June. Between 10 July and 18 August 1943 she acted as a cover and fire support ship during the landing on **Sicily**. In September she took part in the Italian mainland landings at **Taranto** (9-10 September) and **Salerno** (1-19 September). She returned to New York 15 November 1943 and once again steamed to the South Pacific, arriving at Milne Bay, New Guinea, 31 December.

During January-September 1944 she took part in operations along the northern shore of **New Guinea**, including: Madang-Alexishafen bombardment (25-26 January); Humboldt Bay landings (22 April); Wakde-Sawar bombardment (23 30 April), Wakde-Toem landings (1525 May), Biak landings (25 May-10 June), Noewfoor landings (1-2 July); Cape Sansapor landings (27 July-31 August); and the occupation of' Morotai (l0 September). The cruiser moved northward as the battle front advanced into the Philippines taking part in: **Leyte** invasion (21-24 October); **Battle of Surigao Strait** (25 October); **Mindoro** landing (12-17 December), Leyte-Mindoro covering action (26-29 December), **Lingayen Gulf** landings with General D. MacArthur embarked (13 January 1945), Luzon covering force (1-21 January), Bataan-Corregidor occupation (12-17 February) and **Zamboanga** landings (12 March). She then moved to Borneo for the **Tarakan** landings (27 April-8 May). During 2-16 June she carried General MacArthur on a 35,000 mile tour of the Central and Southern Philippines and Brunei Bay, Borneo, and then returned to San Pedro. Calif., arriving 7 July.

The cruiser remained in the San Pedro area undergoing overhaul and training until October. She sailed 3 October for the east coast, arriving at New York 20 October. *Boise* remained there until decommissioned 1 July 1946. She was sold to Argentina 11 January 1951 [as *Nueve De Julio.*]

Boise received ten battle stars for her service in World War II.

USS BOISE CL47

"BRONZE METAL PLAQUE INSTALLED IN THE "ADMIRAL

NIMITZ STATE

HISTORICAL PARK & MUSEUM OF THE PACIFIC WAR"

LOCATED IN

FREDERICKBURA, TEXAS.

IT WILL READ IN PART "DEDICATED TO THE OFFICERS AND

CREW WHO SERVED

IN USS BOISE CL47 DURING WORLD WAR II".

USS BOISE CL47

- ASIATIC—PACIFIC THEATER
  AUGUST 5, 1942 TO SEPTEMBER 15, 1944

Aug. 5, 1942	Lone Tokyo Raid
Sept. 27, 1942	Guadalcanal
Oct. 11-12, 1942	Battle of Cape Esperance
Jan. 25-26, 1944	Alexshafen, New Guinea
April 22, 1944	Humboldt Bay, Dutch New Guinea
April 29-30, 1944	Sawar & Wakde Airdroms, Dutch New Guinea
May 17, 1944	Wakde-Toem Area, Dutch New Guinea
May 27, 1944	Biak Island
July 2, 1944	Noemfoor Island
July 30, 1944	Cape Sansapar, New Guinea
Sept. 15, 1944	Helmahera Island

- FLAGSHIP

Commander in Chief—Southwest Pacific Area
General of the Army—Douglas Mac Arther
January 4-13, 1945—Jun 3-15, 1945

- EUROPEAN THEATER
  JULY 10, 1943 TO SEPTEMBER 16, 1943

July 10-14, 1943	Gela, Sicily
Aug. 12-14, 1943	Cape Calava & Cape Milazzo, Sicily
Aug. 17, 1943	Palini, Italy
Sept. 9, 1943	Taranto, Italy
Sept. 12-16, 1943	Salerno, Italy

- PHILIPPHINE—BORNEDO OPERATIONS
  OCTOBER 20, 1944 TO JUNE 11, 1945

Oct. 20-24, 1944   San Pedro Bay, Leyte Gulf
Oct. 24, 1944   battle of Surigao Straits
Nov. 1, 1944   Heavy Air Attacks, Leyte Gulf
Dec. 15, 1944   San Jose, Mindoro
Jan. 9-14, 1945   Lingayen Gulf, Luzon
Feb. 13-17, 1945   Corregidor and Batoan Peninsula, Luzon
Mar. 8-12, 1945   Zamboanga, Mindanao
May. 1-3, 1945   Tarakan, Borneo
June 8-11, 1945   Brunei Bay, Borneo

- NIGHT SURFACE ENGAGEMENTS

Battle of cape Esperance—11-12 Oct. 1942
Battle of Surigao Straites—25, Oct. 1944

CHAPTER 24

Joined the Naval Reserve November 22, 1942 and traveled to all these places until I was discharged December twelve, nineteen hundred and forty-five.

- Bainbridge, Maryland
- Auburn, Alabama—Radio School
- Norfolk, Virginia—Caught Boise
- Atlantic Ocean
- Mediterranean Sea
- Oran
- Algiers
- Sicily (invasion)
- Gela (invasion)
- Patti
- Palazzo
- Palnui
- Palerno
- Malta (Veletti)
- Italy
- Tarento (Gulf of Tarento)
- Salerno Bay (invasion)
- Bizerta
- Casablanca
- New York, Brooklyn Navy Yard (eighteen days)

- Caribbean Sea
- Panama Canal
- Pacific Ocean
- Balboa (Canal Zone)
- Society Islands (Bora Bora)
- Fyi Islands (Suva)
- New Guinea (Milne Bay)
- Buna
- Madang (bombardment)
- Alexiphafen (bombardment)
- Coral Sea
- Australia (Sydney ten days)
- Hollandia (Dutch New Guinea) eight carriers (invasion)
- Admiralty Islands (Manus Island)
- Wakde Island (invasion)
- Wakde Island (bombardment)
- Biak Island (invasion)
- Numefoor Island (invasion)
- Sansapor (landed Seabees)
- Sydney Australia, August 10, 1944
- Morotai Island (Halmaherra) September 15, 1944
- Philippines (invasion)
- Leyte Samar (invasion)
- Suragio Straits (Surface Battle)
- Mindoro (Philippines invasion)
- Sulu Sea
- Cebu (Philippines)
- Negros (Philippines)
- Luzon (invasion) Laigayen Gulf Philippines

- South China Sea
- Subic Bay
- Bataan (bombardment)
- Corregidor (bombardment)
- Mindanao (Zamboanga)
- (bombardment and invasion five days Philippines)
- Manila (liberty two hours)
- Tarakan (Borneo invasion)
- Brunei Bay Borneo (invasion) (General MacArthur aboard)
- Davao (Philippines)
- Palawan (Philippines)
- Cagayan (Philippines)
- Jolo (Sulu Archipiligao)
- Pearl Harbor (Hawaiian Island)
- California (San Pedro)

When the Captain announced that we were going back to the States, I was overjoyed with happiness. I had not been home in over two years. From May 17, 1945 to June 30, 1945. We anchored at many harbors, but we were getting closer to the States. July 7, 1945 San Pedro, California AT LAST!!!!!!

I was discharged from Bainbridge, Maryland December 12, 1945 and arrived home, East Greenville, Pennsylvania the same day.

HONORABLE DISCHARGE

FROM THE UNITED STATES NAVY

DECEMBER 12, 1945

THE SECRETARY OF THE NAVY
WASHINGTON

January 12, 1946

My dear Mr. Hallman:

I have addressed this letter to reach you after all the formalities of your separation from active service are completed. I have done so because, without formality but as clearly as I know how to say it, I want the Navy's pride in you, which it is my privilege to express, to reach into your civil life and to remain with you always.

You have served in the greatest Navy in the world.

It crushed two enemy fleets at once, receiving their surrenders only four months apart.

It brought our land-based airpower within bombing range of the enemy, and set our ground armies on the beachheads of final victory.

It performed the multitude of tasks necessary to support these military operations.

No other Navy at any time has done so much. For your part in these achievements you deserve to be proud as long as you live. The Nation which you served at a time of crisis will remember you with gratitude.

The best wishes of the Navy go with you into civilian life. Good luck!

Sincerely yours,

James Forrestal

James Forrestal

Mr. Chalmers H. Hallman
349 Main St.
East Greenville, Pennsylvania

LETTER FROM THE SECRETARY OF THE NAVY
WASHINGTON
JANUARY 12, 1946

ABOUT THE AUTHOR

Chalmers H. Hallman, son of Percy and Sadie Heilman Hallman, was born August 9, 1922, in East Greenville, PA.

He participated in all sports football, baseball, tennis, bowling, and golf. He played the Banjo. He also enjoyed playing pool and basketball. He enjoyed hunting and fishing. He spent many weekends dancing at Sunnybrook Ballroom in Pottstown, to the music of Big Name bands, Glenn Miller, Jimmie Dorsey, Tommy Dorsey, Duke Ellington, Harry James.

After graduating from East Greenville High School in 1940, Chalmers joined the Navy in 1942. He survived many frightful close calls during his missions. He was the owner of Sup-Erb Brush Company, in Pennsburg, PA. Chalmers died an untimely death September 9, 2001.

"Lives of great men all remind us
We can make our lives sublime
And, departing, leave behind us
Footprints on the sands of time"

Henry Wadsworth Longfellow

Printed in the United States
131136LV00002B/234/A

9 780595 264254